Beginner's Guide to Writing Powerful Press Releases: Secrets the Pros Use to Command Media Attention

by Mickie Kennedy, Founder & President, eReleases

Contents

Introduction

Years ago, I worked in public relations in Washington, D.C., and I watched as countless small and medium-sized businesses would approach the companies I worked for, asking if we could issue a press release for them. These were businesses that didn't need tens of thousands of dollars pumped into a professionally crafted public relations campaign, so we would have to turn down all of their requests because they couldn't be turned into accounts for us.

Even if these businesses had money that they were willing to spend on a press release, the most basic and essential of public relations tools, every company that I worked for would turn them down because, in their view, dealing with a business that wasn't big enough to bring them significant revenue wasn't worth the effort.

Small businesses and individuals deserve affordable press release distribution.

In 1998 I left that game and started eReleases, a company dedicated to making press release distribution services available and affordable for everyone. I started eReleases because I feel now just as I felt back in D.C., at those large public relations companies — public relations is an essential component for every business, and even small businesses and individuals should have access to affordable, comprehensive press release distribution. That has been our message for more than a decade, and every year that message resonates more and more strongly with our customers.

We at eReleases believe that press releases are for everyone. Every business — from giant, multi-national conglomerates to small, one-person operations — has the ability to issue a press release. And one of the most beautiful things about the way press releases are distributed today is that every press release is practically equal. Newswire distribution is a wonderfully democratic system that puts a press release from a conglomerate and a press release from a one-person operation on equal footing. And on this equal playing field, the primary factor that could separate a small business' press release from a conglomerate's is the way that it is written.

For years, people have been coming to eReleases with a common problem: They want to use press releases, but they don't know how to write them. We have done what we could to help, giving advice, editing drafts, or just referring them to our press release writing services if necessary. And while we don't mind writing press releases for customers, we feel that the person who is best-suited to be in control of your company's PR efforts is you.

I know that writing a press release for the first time can be intimidating, but the truth is, writing a professional press release is really quite easy. All it takes is a little know-how. And that is why I wrote this book.

What you have now is an all-in-one guide to go from being a complete novice to a writer of professional-grade press releases. Each of the four sections in this book focuses on a specific area of press releases so that you can have a robust understanding of what they are and how they operate as part of a larger public relations campaign.

The first section is a basic introduction and overview of press release writing and distribution. The second section focuses on the individual components of a press release, with each chapter addressing a single press release element in depth. The third section examines a newer sub-set of public relations known as an SEO press release. Finally, the fourth section discusses the reality and expectations for releasing a press release, as well as what to do and expect after you have started distributing press releases.

With the knowledge and guidelines contained within this book, you will have vital tools empowering you to write confidently and use press releases beneficially as the cornerstone of any future public relations endeavor.

Yours Truly,

Mickie Kennedy

Founder & President

eReleases Press Release Services

Section 1:
Press Releases 101

Chapter 1

For Immediate Release:

The History of the Press Release

The Origin of the Press Release and Its Importance to Public Relations

Have you ever heard the story of how a young man named Ivy Lee responded to a tragedy that took the lives of more than 50 people and used it to create what would become a mainstay of any public relations effort? Don't worry if you haven't. The truth is that most public relations practitioners haven't either.

According to public relations lore, the press release was born following a train wreck on October 28, 1906, in Atlantic City, N.J., that left more than 50 people dead.

The train was owned by Pennsylvania Railroad, one of Ivy Lee's clients. In response to the disaster, he convinced the railroad to issue a statement about what had transpired. In doing so, he set in motion a practice for companies to address issues important to them, or, in the case of the railroad, to offer an explanation of what had happened. The *New York Times* was said to have been so impressed by Lee's release that the newspaper printed it exactly as Lee had written it. Although it's rare for media outlets to use press releases verbatim these days, they still often act as a starting point for a journalist to create a story.

When Ivy Lee created what is widely believed to be the first press release, he established an invaluable component to any public relations campaign. The times and technology may have changed, but there are several things a press release can accomplish that make its use as relevant today as when Lee was alive:

- ✓ A press release can quickly and effectively share information about an event, product, campaign promise, meeting, or host of other events — any situation in which the same information needs to reach everyone.

- ✓ A press release provides an opportunity for you to share your take on why a product is special, respond to claims made by others, explain why your organization is important, etc., rather than only allowing others to define you.

✓ A press release offers the best opportunity for you to guarantee that information about a product, statement of a position, dates and times of an event, etc., are shared correctly with the public.

Press releases remain an important tool for attracting the attention of the news media.

More than 100 years after Lee's innovation, press releases remain an important tool for attracting the attention of the news media to a newsworthy item of information. Also known as news releases or media releases, press releases are documents in a specific format and are now used for a variety of purposes that include:

1. Providing news in situations when a company needs to address an issue, respond to a crisis, and/or share general information.

2. Announcements by individuals intending to seek elected office or responses by candidates to allegations made against them.

3. A company announcing a new or improved product/service.

4. A company announcing a boom in sales or response to accusations against them.

5. The sharing of data, statistics, tips, trends, perspectives or other pertinent information that would be of interest to a particular industry.

6. The announcement of a press conference or an upcoming event.

7. An author or publisher sharing information about the release of a new book.

8. Information from artists sharing news about their latest album, movie, showing, etc.

The list of uses for press releases has grown over the years, and with it there has also been an evolution in the forms of press releases — each of which serves a different purpose.

Before turning to the types of releases, I want to present a modern-day example of a press release so you know exactly what we are talking about. Some people have heard they should be sending releases to get media attention, but they have never actually seen what they look like. So here is a typical example.

ScienceResearch.com Debuts as the World's Most Comprehensive Deep Web Science Search Engine

SANTA FE, N.M., June 15, 20xx — ScienceResearch.com, now the world's most comprehensive Deep Web science search engine, provides a single point of access to over 400 high-quality publicly searchable science and technology collections with a new, robust user interface specifically designed for advanced scientific research. Built with scalability in mind, in terms of collections searched in parallel and number of concurrent users, ScienceResearch.com is deployed at an Amazon Cloud Computing Data Center. Originally released in 2005 as a search engine focused on providing access to publicly searchable journal literature, ScienceResearch.com now boasts a greatly expanded set of searchable collections and Deep Web Technologies' next-generation federated search engine, helping researchers (at any level) find accurate results for their science and technology research.

ScienceResearch.com is Web 2.0-based and makes available a number of advanced capabilities, including relevance ranking, clustering and the ability to select results of interest and e-mail them to a colleague or export them to citation management software such as EndNote or RefWorks. It searches all the collections in real-time. "Our goal is to make more science research available to more individuals than any other portal," said Abe Lederman, President and CTO of Deep Web Technologies. "We want to facilitate scientific discovery. The moment information is published in any of these deep web collections, it can be found by interested researchers."

The key idea behind ScienceResearch.com is to promote the discovery of information by searching authoritative, "deep web" collections of information from around the world. These collections include publicly available collections as well as subscription or premium resources that are publicly searchable. Users of ScienceResearch.com will find that a lot of the information in these collections is unavailable from the popular search engines, since they cannot index these "deep web" resources.

Next-generation federated search technology has become a strategic necessity for serious researchers, corporations and other professionals where finding the needle-in-the-hay-stack is critical to their success.

ScienceResearch.com is divided into 15 categories, including Chemistry, Earth and Environmental Sciences, Health and Medicine and Physics. Categories have also been created for Science News and Patents. Users can search any number of categories, searching all collections within the categories selected, or choose specific collections within a category to narrow their search. "Featured collections" are included, which search major science search portals including Science.gov, WorldWideScience.org and the E-Print Network. ScienceResearch.com's categories are managed by volunteer moderators who want to help the ScienceResearch.com team select the best, most authoritative collections to include in each category. ScienceResearch.com is seeking moderators for several categories.

"We hope that ScienceResearch.com will help to accelerate scientific discovery around the world," commented Lederman. "This portal promotes the cross-fertilization of ideas and theories among researchers in different fields through the simultaneous search of hundreds of important collections that a researcher might not otherwise find."

Mr. Lederman will be featuring ScienceResearch.com in his contributed paper at the Special Libraries Association Centennial conference in Washington, DC this June 20xx. His paper, entitled "Science Research: Journey to 10,000 Sources," is available on the SLA website.

About Deep Web Technologies

Deep Web Technologies (http://www.deepwebtech.com) creates custom, sophisticated federated search solutions for clients who demand precise, accurate results. The tool of choice when needing to access the deep web, federated search performs real-time, parallel searches of multiple information sources, merging the results into one page. Serving Fortune 500 companies, the Science.gov Alliance (http://www.science.gov), the U.S. Dept. of Energy, the Dept. of Defense, Scitopia.org (http://www.scitopia.org), Nutrition.gov, WorldWideScience.org (http://www.worldwidescience.org) and a variety of other customers and partners, Deep Web Technologies has built a reputation as the "researcher's choice" for its advanced, agile information discovery tools.

Media contact:

Darcy Pedersen

darcy@deepwebtech.com or 505-820-0301 x233

# # #

The Evolution of the Press Release and Its Different Functions

Over the years, both the significance and purpose of press releases have matured to become a cornerstone of the public relations world; at the same time, the forms that press releases take have also changed to fit specific needs. Now there are actually many different types of releases.

Although they are all called press releases, there are several different types of releases, named according to their function, that have been used over the years. They include:

- **Standard release.** The standard release is much like the one first issued by Lee in 1906 and is still used by organizations today to share information. Along the way certain things have been updated, like the importance of adding specific contact information, boilerplates (the section headed "About Deep Web Technologies" in the sample press release above), and standing logos that make the release stand out from others.

- **Media advisory.** The media advisory was created not so much to share information as it was to announce another mainstay of public relations — the press conference. The media advisory was envisioned as a means of generating excitement about a press conference in which details about anything from the opening of a new business to the unveiling of a new product would be announced. Rather than actually sharing information, a media advisory is more of a hook to get the media interested in attending a press conference or event, with the details to follow.

- **Embargoed release.** Eventually, it was realized that embargoed releases could be used by organizations to share information more effectively. An embargoed release contains information such as the exact text of a speech, data, sales figures, etc. that is sent to a media source prior to a press conference or announcement. It is primarily used to assure that detailed or complicated information is shared accurately, with the understanding that it's not to be used until after a specific date, time, or event that is indicated at the top of the release.

While embargoed releases are still used, due to the high visibility of releases and the incredible speed at which information now travels, it is getting harder and harder to maintain an embargo and prevent information from leaking.

One other important change in recent years is that with the widespread usage of the Internet, press releases are now at least partially a tool for communicating with the general public or specialized niches as well as with the representatives of newspapers, magazines, radio and television. Bloggers and industry opinion leaders who are not traditional journalists often regularly read press releases to keep up with what's new in their areas of interest. These thought leaders can be even more influential than traditional media.

Press releases are now at least partially a tool for communicating with the general public.

Prior to the Internet, it would be rare for someone not in the news business to be exposed to a press release. But because press releases are now archived on the web, often show up in search engine results and may be streamed on many news sites and industry portals, people with no journalistic training may very well run across your press release and click through to learn more about your organization, event or product. Indeed, in Section 3 of this guide, I explain how releases can be an important component of your social media efforts.

The Evolution of Sending Press Releases

Technology has had a major impact on the way press releases reach their destination by making distribution more efficient and opening up the possibility of immediate delivery. For recipients, technology has made it easier for them to receive a release in a timely manner, which greatly improves the chances of it being used.

Because of the rapid advancement of technology, tools that were never specifically envisioned for press releases have now vastly improved how releases are disseminated. To get a sense of this advancement, let's take a look back at how press releases reached their destination prior to and following the 1970s.

Before the 1970s

For more than half a century, the only methods for transmitting a press release were delivery in person, dictation over the phone or sending it through the mail. In 1954, the founding of PR Newswire made it possible to broadcast releases through teletype machines, which would clack out the text of releases letter by letter in major newsrooms.

The founding of PR Newswire made it possible to broadcast releases more quickly.

All of these delivery methods produced several inefficiencies:

1. **Timeliness.** Information included in releases might be urgent, but getting them to their recipients often took hours when hand-delivered, or days when sent by mail. Although PR Newswire and other similar services could get a story to the news media quickly, even the most well-established corporations lacked technology to get the releases equally quickly to the newswire company or directly to the news media.

2. **Reaching the right individual.** Except when hand-delivered to the right person or mailed in an envelope addressed to a certain reporter or editor, it was challenging to get a press release to its intended recipient. The teletype service got press releases into the newsroom, but from there it was up to the news outlet to distribute the news items to whoever covered business, sports or fashion.

3. **The need for retyping.** While it was hoped that journalists and other distributors were diligent in accurately transcribing information from a release, there was a constant danger of mistakes creeping in. Dates might be copied inaccurately, key words could be left out of statements, names could be misspelled, and a host of other problems could result in data

being conveyed wrongly in the transition from a typed release to the news.

The 1970s saw a revolution in how information was shared that benefited not only public relations, but almost every profession. Key among those changes was the facsimile (fax) machine, which was followed by computer stations and the Internet.

With each new technology, public relations practitioners were able to guard more effectively against the three factors that had previously hindered them in their work while simultaneously taking their profession into bold new directions.

After the 1970s

Ivy Lee had a good thing going with his press release, but changes in communication and computer technology, which improved delivery time and functionality, meant that PR professionals had to innovate and adapt.

With changes in communication and computer technology, PR professionals had to innovate and adapt.

Let's look at some of those innovations, along with their shortcomings and improved processes:

Fax Machines

Imagine the ability for someone in an office in New York City to send a document to someone in Los Angeles in a matter of minutes, and for the recipient to see the way the original document looked. While not a particularly impressive feat now, up until the 1970s, such a thing was beyond comprehension to most people. The introduction of the fax machine revolutionized business communications, forever changing the way that businesses operate. As a result, the superiority of sending press releases by fax was quickly recognized.

Problem solved: Timeliness. Rather than having to wait hours or days for a press release that was hand-delivered or sent by mail, a release could reach its destination in minutes. This technology was cheaper, faster and more democratic than the teletype machines, since fax transmission worked through telephone lines rather than through separate, dedicated lines.

Limitations: Fax machines definitely improved the time in which a release could reach its general destination, but there were still limitations that included:

1. Reaching the right recipient. Many organizations had only one fax machine, with the result that while the release might arrive at its intended destination, it would arrive at a central distribution

point rather than on the desk of the appropriate editor.

2. Possibility of error. Releases sent by the first fax machines were often blurry and difficult to read. This still created the possibility for errors as information had to be copied and retyped by journalists.

3. Photographs, logos, charts and other visual information did not come through clearly at the destination.

4. Lengthy releases tended to pile up, cluttering the desks of those who received them.

Computer Stations

In the 1970s, digital technology began to show up in newsrooms, with computer news terminals replacing the teletype machines as a means of sending stories quickly from one news organization to another and from press release distribution services to newsrooms. However, these computers were not common at smaller newspapers or broadcast outlets. Magazines were more likely to have fax machines than computer terminals.

Since computer systems were very large and expensive, terminals had to be shared by many people. News organizations might therefore print incoming news on dot-matrix printers and spread it around the office on paper rather than working on the digital files.

As more and more editors and reporters learned how to perform electronic word processing and were given their own terminal to work on, news personnel gradually became able to take a digitally received press release and transform it into an article without retyping it from scratch.

However, digitally received material could not be automatically routed to the appropriate news department.

E-mail

Just as fax machines forever revolutionized how information was shared, e-mail furthered the process. Not only was it possible to deliver a press release in minutes, e-mail made it possible for the information to go directly to the intended recipient.

Sending press releases by e-mail also allowed for lengthier releases, links to articles, and the inclusion of graphics, photographs, and data. Because the information arrived on the recipient's computer, transferring information to another document was as simple as copying and pasting it.

Problems solved: E-mail not only expanded the rapid delivery available through fax and electronic transmission to the newsroom, it also assured a release would reach the desktop of a particular recipient without cluttering desks.

Limitations: E-mail can be easily abused. Spam and off-topic releases clog up inboxes or lead to larger problems. Multi-megabyte photographs and large PDFs also can jam journalist inboxes and lead to considerable frustration. And with the frequent shuffling of personnel at news organizations, e-mail addresses can go out of date. Some news organizations use functional or departmental rather than personal e-mail addresses (i.e., sports@eveningnews.com rather than lizab@eveningnews.com), which again raises the need for someone to route the incoming e-mail to the right individuals.

The World Wide Web

Of course, e-mail would not be possible without the Internet. But the development of the World Wide Web also meant that organizations could post press releases for an indefinite period as a statement of record on their website.

Because of the Internet, organizations now have online documentation of the launching of new products, new personnel and events, as well as their positions on issues. Along with easy viewing from any computer connected to the Internet, the Web offers the opportunity for anyone to view the releases as originally written in their entirety, rather than in the transformed stories in which various media organizations may have used the information.

The Web offers the opportunity for anyone to view the releases as originally written in their entirety.

Posting releases to an organization's website also allowed it to list releases by the year of distribution or under different subject headings to enable ease of access by the public in determining an organization's position regarding various issues.

Web 2.0

Since 2000 or so, press releases have acquired multi-media capabilities, so that they may be accompanied by photographs, diagrams, other images and audio or video files.

Press releases also began to become integrated into the fabric of social media interchanges. It's now possible to post or link to releases from a Facebook or Myspace page, talk about them on a discussion board, refer people to a release from a blog or Twitter post, bookmark it for others or syndicate it through RSS feeds. (We will turn to Web 2.0 publicity methods in Section 3.)

Many press releases now show up in Google News exactly the way the company wrote them, mixed together with journalist-written stories from famous news organizations. Press releases may also get syndicated to topical news sites, where anyone interested in what's happening in, let's say, high finance, pet news or elementary education can read them.

In short, while press releases still provide a means of interesting the media in your story, they now offer much, much more.

Newswires

Perhaps the most important advance in the history of press release distribution was the introduction of the newswire. There are many different histories and purposes for the numerous newswires that are out there, and going into them in detail would require a book unto itself.

Dating back to 1954 with the launch of PR Newswire, a newswire is a news delivery system that allows for a controlled, efficient, central distribution of news. With a newswire, a business just has to send a press release to the wire, and the wire will then distribute it directly to the newsrooms of thousands of media outlets, including radio, TV, and newspapers. Using a newswire eliminates the need for a company to maintain their own media lists and then to mail, hand-deliver, fax or e-mail press releases to them.

Media outlets also often trust the material they receive from the newswires more than something arriving on a company letterhead. After all, it is easy to fake a logo and write a fraudulent release that might affect a company's stock price or image. The same goes for today's faxed or e-mailed press releases. Indeed, the newswires have a series of safeguards in place to help prevent fraudulent releases purporting to be from or about publicly traded companies from being distributed.

Media outlets trust the material they receive from the newswires more than other material.

Originally newswires delivered stories to the media using teletype machines. Then the releases would get printed out on dot-matrix printers in the newsroom. Later, newsrooms would have a primitive computer system with shared terminals, and releases would be delivered to those. More recently, the newswires use the Internet to get releases to journalists. Reporters and editors working for a news organization log into the newswire on their company's intranet, where they have the ability to customize exactly which categories of releases they want to see and which they prefer not to see.

Individual journalists can also request that the newswires fax or e-mail them releases in the categories that they specify. These categories sometimes accommodate very narrow distinctions, such as video gaming vs. online gaming. Journalists can also request releases according to keywords they contain. For instance, someone who covers the rivalry between Coca-Cola and Pepsi would request all releases containing "Coca-Cola," "Coke," "Pepsi," etc.

In addition, the newswires deliver their releases on the web in the form of RSS feeds in hundreds of categories that automatically place their content on various websites, with the latest material on top. Members of the general public can also subscribe to the newsfeeds that interest them and read them on their desktop.

Both journalists and members of the general public can also find press releases on conglomerated news sites such as Google News or Yahoo News, where press releases may show up alongside stories from news organizations when viewing a particular category of news or performing a keyword search.

On conglomerated news sites, press releases may show up alongside stories from news organizations.

How Does it Work?

Though the technology of distribution has changed drastically over the decades, this is how the wire feed works today: Business X decides to distribute a press release about its new product. Since this product is some new, fantastic computer hardware that drastically reduces greenhouse gases, when the business sends its press release to the wire, the release will be categorized according to the topics that it addresses, in this case in categories like Computer Hardware, New Products, and Environmental Issues. Then it will be posted to the wire.

Almost every journalist for TV, newspapers, or radio reads the wires every day for story ideas, feature leads, you name it. But most journalists don't report on everything; they have distinct topics that they write about and they focus mostly on them. So when journalists start work in the morning, from their computer they log into the wire section of their organization's intranet, where all the press releases are listed under categories, and read the headlines in the categories that apply to them.

So for the previous example of the new computer hardware, those journalists who cover the categories of Computer Hardware, New Products, and Environmental Issues log in, and among the other press releases in those respective categories, they see Business X's release about its amazing new product. The release's information is now in the hands of the journalists to do with it what they will. Hopefully they will write a big article about it!

Different Newswires

Most people, when they hear the word "newswire," think of the Associated Press (AP), Reuters, or United Press International (UPI). These are vastly different from the commercial newswires that deal with press releases. Their delivery method is similar, but the AP deals solely in news stories written by AP journalists so that they can be reprinted in other newspapers. AP, Reuters, and UPI license their content to newspapers, media outlets, and websites. While they receive press releases and monitor newswires that post press releases, they transform press releases into actual stories. Press releases are written by publicists for journalists rather than by journalists for consumers. You can think of press releases as the raw material for news stories. When they hit the mark, they get transformed into news stories.

When it comes to distributing press releases to journalists, there are four main wires: PR Newswire, Business Wire, Marketwire, and GlobeNewswire. Of the four, PR Newswire is the oldest and largest, followed by Business Wire. These two are often referred to as the Tier 1 wires because journalists appear to use and respect them the most. Marketwire and GlobeNewswire, often referred to as the Tier 2 wires, tend to specialize in news about publicly traded companies and are good at reaching investors and stock pickers.

The four main wires are often referred to as the Tier 1 wires.

The Tier 1 wires charge in the range of $800 — $1,000 for national distribution of a 500-word press release, while the Tier 2 wires charge around half of that. As you might expect from the difference in prices, the Tier 1 newswires have a greater reach with journalists and online databases than the Tier 2 wires.

There is absolutely no benefit to putting out the same release over multiple wires. In most cases, the same journalists and major media outlets will receive a press release no matter which wire it is distributed over.

Other companies that distribute releases may have a subcontracting relationship with a Tier 1 or Tier 2 newswire. And still other press release distribution companies primarily just post releases on the Web so that they can be indexed by search engines and found there by journalists or the general public.

Why Press Releases Are Necessary

Just as Ivy Lee recognized the need for Pennsylvania Railroad to make a statement explaining the train wreck that occurred in 1906, businesses large and small, entrepreneurs and other individuals have come to realize the need to send press releases out into the world.

Not only did press releases become the premier way to distribute uniform, accurate information for businesses, it also became the standard way to distribute all kinds of information of interest. And most importantly, a press release is the best way to present information as factual content. Countless times every day people are bombarded by advertisements, and while advertisements do work to an extent, many of us have a habit of tuning them out as much as possible. There is an insincerity to advertising that instantly puts many people off — and on the defensive.

Content, however, is another story. People crave content. Content is what we choose to fill our time with, be it magazines, newspapers, websites, or what have you. And if content is what people want to consume, you'd be a bad businessperson if you didn't want your information to become the content that people want to consume.

Journalists have a rough job because they have to create content constantly. People on the radio need something to talk about for hours on end, and newspaper editors stare down dozens of empty newspaper pages that they have to fill each day. All of this content has to come from somewhere, so it might as well come from you. If a business is regularly putting out press releases about noteworthy subjects, like the hiring of a new CEO, a new product, or a list of tips from an insider, then that has the potential to become journalistic content. If it is of interest, and it has the potential to fill up space, time, or even just flesh out a story that was already in the works, the benefit of that exposure can be enormous.

Journalists have to create content constantly.

From an economic standpoint, press releases benefit business. For many prominent news magazines, a quarter-page advertisement could top $80,000. But if a press release leads to a quarter-page write-up, not only will it have cost significantly less than buying ad space, the credibility and readership that comes from the information being used as content will far surpass the impact an advertisement could have. In fact, news has three times more credibility and six times more readership than paid advertising of equivalent size, according to Starch

Research.

The media can even benefit economically from press releases because they can use the additional pages of content developed from press releases to sell additional advertising space. It's a win-win situation.

Chapter 2

Anatomy of the Press Release

Throughout this book you will see one concept frequently emphasized because it's so basic and essential that it bears repeating as many times as possible. This prevailing concept is that press releases are a first step: They are an introduction, a handshake, a single component of a larger, multifaceted public relations campaign. In function, that is what a press release is, but let's take a step back for a moment and review the true basics of a press release.

A press release is not an advertisement and not an article.

A press release is a document that announces newsworthy information about a business to members of the press. It is not an advertisement. It is not an article similar to one you would read in a newspaper. It is a succinct communication with the media concerning a business's noteworthy events or positions. That could include everything from the announcement of a merger or new hire, to a top ten list of insider tips compiled by an expert in a business.

Keep in mind that a press release is intended for the media. It is everyone's hope that a release, in the hands of the media, will lead to coverage of some kind, which will in turn bring added business and attention to a company, but this is never guaranteed. That is why a press release is just a first step and must be part of a larger public relations picture. If you want more consistent coverage, there has to be a consistent relationship between you, the media, your community, and your industry. Press releases can play an integral role in this process. The details surrounding this appear in later chapters.

For now, though, it's best to focus on the basic elements of a press release. Now that we know that a press release is something that is used to get media attention, let's move to an outline of the foundations of effective press release writing.

Building a Press Release

No two press releases are the same, but they should all share similarities. While it's worthwhile to make a press release stand out, all press releases should include a headline, dateline, opening paragraph, body paragraphs, boilerplate and contact information. Let's go through those elements one by one.

Headline

Because of its prominence and position, the headline is the first thing the media will read. Most people, even journalists, decide to read or skip a press release based on the headline alone. Because of that, the headline is without a doubt the single most important component of a press release.

A headline has to grab people's attention as well as be informative about the content of a release. Knowing how important headlines are, many people try and write sensational headlines that all but demand to be read, but that is the exact wrong thing to do. The best headlines are simple, one-sentence explanations of a press release's purpose and origin. If the information in a press release is newsworthy, then it will sell itself. No sensationalism is needed. As you advance in your press release writing skills, you can learn the subtle art of adding pizzazz to a headline while maintaining its objective integrity.

Many people add a subhead to the press release. A subhead is an additional sentence that provides newsworthy details that either create a new hook or angle for the media or supports the previous hook given in the headline. A subhead is not required and many times not needed in a press release. It is important that the subhead not deflate or steal elements that would be best left for the opening paragraph. The novice press release writer is best to forget the subhead until they've honed the basic press release writing skills.

Dateline

A dateline is a very simple element that plainly states when and from where a press release originated. Datelines appear in the first line of a press release, before the actual release begins, and they list a city and state then the date when a press release is issued. There are some peculiarities to the formatting of this, though, which will be discussed later. But for the time being, just writing your city and state the way you would for your address is fine.

Opening Paragraph

The opening paragraph is the second most important part of a press release, right after the headline. Also like the headline, the opening paragraph has the function of capturing and holding people's attention while informing them of the important details in a release.

This first paragraph can often be thought of as an "executive summary" to a press release because it will be skimmed by readers trying to see if reading the whole release is worth their time. Again, do not make this sensational in an attempt to keep people interested. Sticking to the important information will work just fine. Many people find that, when trying to write this paragraph, it is best to skip it at first, write the rest of the press release, and then write the opening paragraph, highlighting only the most important, newsworthy information that is discussed in the body.

Body Paragraphs

The paragraphs that comprise the body are the meat of the press release. There are usually three to five paragraphs in the body that flesh out information so that readers can have a fully nuanced understanding of what the press release is announcing.

There aren't really any hard and fast rules to abide by for these paragraphs. Simply state what needs to be said in a manner that is both fluid and understandable. It is important that each paragraph builds upon the previous paragraph(s) and that they in their entirety support and fully describe the headline and opening paragraph.

Boilerplate

Of all these listed elements, this is the only one that is preferred but optional. A boilerplate is a short paragraph that provides a little background information about the company or person issuing a press release. That way anyone reading a press release issued by an unfamiliar person or company can have a basic understanding of the person or company's credentials without having to do additional research.

A boilerplate is preferred but optional.

Boilerplates are made to be standardized paragraphs that can be used in many situations, and most large companies position them at the end of every press release. But most small businesses leave them off to help save space. They are preferable to include because they help reporters understand basic background about the press release's source, and they do help reinforce name and brand recognition. There are no rules stating that you have to have one. However, once you have written one, you can recycle it again and again in future press releases.

Contact Information

Contact information should be the last entry in a press release. The information provided should be for an individual press contact. The press contact should be someone who can speak for the company and who can answer any questions that the press may have.

The press would rather have only one contact.

Ideally, contact information should include a name, that person's title, phone number, e-mail address, and the company's website. Optionally, a fax number, after-hours numbers, and additional contacts can be included as well. The press would rather have only one contact, however, so use multiple ones only if it is necessary and there are clearly defined reasons for each contact.

Many individuals still try to write the press contact at the top of the press release. This is a holdover from the old telegraph days, and even from the heyday of faxing, when it was critical to position the information at the top in case the transmission was cut off. That is not an issue with newswire transmission, and press contact information will automatically move down to the foot of the release during a newswire's editorial review.

The 5 Ws

Press releases can be ineffective in how they convey information, which is why focus is paramount in any public relations effort. After the essential elements that were just outlined, focus is the next most important factor.

A public relations executive once commented that losing focus is the biggest mistake beginners make when they write press releases: "They know what they want to say, they even know how to say it, but they don't take the time to review the release to make sure they've explained the information in a manner that will spark the interest of those reading the release."

Journalists are taught to remember the 5 Ws (what, who, where, when, and why or how) when writing in order to create focus and keep readers' interested in a story. The 5 Ws are just as relevant in public relations in order to spark people's interest and keep the writer focused on the press release's most important information.

Recipients should know what a release is about right up front.

Including the 5 Ws early in the body of a press release, especially in the headline and opening paragraph, is important so that recipients know what a release is about right up front and don't have to read the entire release before realizing why they should care. Clearly addressing relevant information is crucial to ensuring that journalists are attracted to the information in the press release and keep reading.

The 5 Ws include:

Get to the point early.

1. **What.** A press release shouldn't be rambling; get to the point early so readers can quickly determine the release's relevance. Both the headline and opening paragraph should include what's important about your information. Remember:

   - Do take time to read the release and ask yourself whether importance and relevance could easily be determined if you were the recipient and reading the information for the first time.

   - Don't write a press release that attempts to be sensational or cute. Doing so results in relevant information being buried deep in the release. Being coy only guarantees that your release will be ignored. Clearly state all assertions and conclusions.

2. **Who.** Identify the source of the press release as well as those who will be affected by the information in your release.

   Let's take a look at a headline and an opening excerpt from a press release that fails to identify its target audience or make the point of the release clear.

   Government Announces Revenue Shortfalls May Reduce Services

   NEW YORK, Oct. 15, 20xx — Due to an unexpected fall in revenue, certain services will have to be cut back in the coming year. The mayor's office made the announcement this morning after mounting reports of economic turmoil.

   Neither the headline nor the opening sentences addresses the basics of the information. There is no indication of where this is an issue, who it will affect, or how widespread the problem is. Even though the problem is outlined, the crucial information is not given. This is unlike the following example, which has been corrected.

   New York City Government to Experience Reduction in Civil Services Due to Drop in Revenue

   NEW YORK, Oct. 15 20xx — New York City Mayor Michael Bloomberg announced this morning that due to a lack of revenue from drops in tourism, funding to many civil programs will have to be cut back over the next year. The changes are likely to affect those who rely on publicly funded services like schools and veteran's hospitals.

The corrected excerpt more immediately addresses the 5 Ws and gives readers the most important information right away.

3. **Where.** The *where* in a release isn't only about the location where something occurred, but also the areas that the information discussed will influence. First, though, let's look at a few examples of things to check for in terms of location:

   - Both the headline and opening paragraph of a press release should make it easy to determine where an event is being held or announcement will be made.

   - Information about where to find additional facts that are too long or involved to include in a release should be easy to locate.

   - Specific locations that have been or will be affected by the information in a release should be identified. An example would be: If there is a release on how parts of a street will be without power, it should specifically mention the blocks that will be affected.

   But, as mentioned above, clarifying the *where* of a press release also includes addressing areas such as:

   - Where will the new offices be built?

   - Where will the benefits of a program be most recognized?

4. **When.** As with where, explaining *when* in a release not only includes dates and times, but also time periods. Let's start by examining the importance of reviewing details related to time:

   - Make sure your release doesn't read "Tuesday, July 12," when the twelfth of July is a Wednesday.

   - Times shouldn't be formatted in multiple ways throughout the release, like writing a date "12 July" in one place, "July 12th" later, and then "7/12" as well.

   - Also make sure the release specifies whether an event or announcement is scheduled for 7:30 a.m. or 7:30 p.m.

   - Time zones can be a good idea also as most press releases now gain national, if not global, exposure.

When can also answer more general or conditional timing questions, such as:

- When can employees expect to benefit from a new initiative?

- When can fans of a recording artist purchase their latest album?

- When will the price change take effect?

- When the fundraiser is over, then the project will begin.

5. **Why.** If addressed correctly, the *what, who, where,* and *when* in the text should point to why the information in a press release is important. But the *why* should still be specifically addressed. Just as the headline and opening paragraph of a press release should grab the attention of those receiving it, subsequent paragraphs should build on and reinforce the *why.*

Some Thoughts About Making Sure Everything Comes Together

Even after the 5 Ws have been addressed and the essential elements are brought together, the work of creating an effective press release is far from finished. Think of the 5 Ws as the ingredients in a recipe: Every good chef knows that the most delicious creations can be made only by combining the best ingredients in just the right way.

The 5 Ws help a press release be brief and to the point.

Because a press release is the first step in contacting the media about an event or product, it represents the best chance of garnering coverage, so assuring your press release jumps out from the pack is essential. The 5 Ws can help make sure that successful press releases are brief, to the point, and make important information easy to find. Failure to do this means a press release may be quickly discarded.

Short and Sweet

Press releases aren't meant to be epic works of fiction or sprawling histories. They are a conveyance of information, and they preferably focus on only one newsworthy bit of information at a time. So when writing a release, it's best to remember the acronym K.I.S.S., which stands for "Keep It Short, Stupid!"

K.I.S.S. is also known as "Keep It Simple, Stupid," but no matter how you define it, the message is the same. When sending a press release, get right to the point.

Since "short" can sometimes be open to interpretation, here is a guideline to live by: From start to finish, press releases should be 400-500 words or fewer.

This isn't necessarily an arbitrary figure. Editors and reporters themselves have indicated that 350-500 words is a comfortable, one-sitting reading range. In practical terms, 350-500 words translates to roughly a page in a standard word-processor document. Most wire services have adopted this model and limit their press releases to 400 words without penalty. Above 400 words, you will be levied overage charges. This is a fairly strict policy, so don't be surprised to see an extra charge tagged onto your bill because you thought 410 words was close enough.

That's not to say that press releases that go over 400 words are indefensible. In fact, eReleases doesn't charge for extra words until a press release reaches 500 words. eReleases recognizes that those extra 100 words can make all the difference in the right situations. Sometimes it is just not possible get everything in under a word limit, but under no circumstances should a press release ever be longer than the equivalent of two word-processor pages.

If you are on the fence on whether or not some information you have in a release is worth the extra cost to retain, there are some other things to consider. A press release that is too detailed, rambles, or is vague can be ineffective for two reasons:

1. It's difficult to understand the importance of information in the release.
2. Important information is buried deep in the release.

Either scenario is likely to cause a journalist to stop reading or skip a press release entirely. So if a release is long, double-check that everything in it is absolutely necessary. Multiple pages aren't preferable, but it does happen on occasion when a press release contains, for example, large collections of data, earnings figures, or the full text of a speech. In such cases, though, it is best to make a one-page release that is largely stand-alone, but include a link where the extra information can be viewed online.

Be careful not to lose vital information while trying to be concise. Sometimes edits can lead to the unintended loss of important information, either because it was entirely removed or condensed to the point of obfuscation. When important information is lost or unintelligible, readers on deadline will simply move on to the next press release instead of calling or e-mailing for clarification.

And Did You Remember to Include...?

Once the 5 Ws have been addressed, an accurate headline is written, and an opening paragraph is created, you're home free, right?

Wrong!

The work of creating an effective press release is only just beginning, even after these items have been addressed. While the basics are necessary to make a press release that is relevant and accessible, the release also has to be written in a convincing tone that accentuates the importance of the information and makes people take it seriously. Unlike the 5 Ws, this is more art than science.

We'll conclude this chapter with a press release checklist. Novice public relations professionals would do well to keep this checklist handy and reference it for the items that should and shouldn't be included in most press releases.

Press Release Dos and Don'ts: a Checklist

Form

❏ Is your headline brief, comprehensive, and attention-grabbing?

❏ If you have a subhead after the headline, is it written concisely?

❏ Is your dateline written properly?

❏ Does your opening paragraph summarize the most important information in your press release?

❏ Are your body paragraphs informative and written concisely?

❏ Do you list the appropriate contact information?

❏ Does your release include a call to action — what you would like the reader of the release to do next?

❏ Is your release written in the third person (he/she/it/they), using the first person (I) only for quotes, and completely omitting the second person (you)?

❏ Has your release been proofread for grammar, punctuation, spelling, consistency, and usage at least twice, preferably by readers who are unfamiliar with the material?

❏ Are all URLs and hyperlinks within the text properly configured?

❏ Is your entire press release between 350 and 500 words?

❏ Are trademarks and company/product names represented consistently?

❏ Is your press release written in clear, concise language?

Substance

❏ Is your press release newsworthy? Does it convey useful information relevant to your target audience?

❏ Does your press release read like an advertisement (bad) or a news story (good)?

❏ Does it avoid sensationalism, gimmickry, and cuteness?

❏ Do your quotes add a human element and relevant information to your press release, rather than just restating the facts?

❏ Does your release refrain from making outrageous claims?

❏ Can everything in your release be documented or substantiated?

❏ Does your release steer clear of anything that would be offensive to your audience?

❏ Is it clear who is issuing the press release?

❏ Does your release stay focused, avoiding irrelevant details?

❏ If your press release references legal issues, public companies, or celebrities, have you checked that it complies with the newswire's standards?

❏ Is your press release written for journalists and your target audience?

Chapter 3

The Write Way:

Guidelines for Press Release Writing

Words Can Be So Intimidating

We know. You don't have to tell us. It's something we've heard countless times before: You don't know how to write a press release. You haven't really written anything since you were in school and you didn't like it then. You doubt that anything you write will even be noticed since you don't think that it can hold a candle to something written by a professional. We've heard it all. But if that were truly the case, we wouldn't be writing this book for you, now would we?

Anyone can sit down and write a truly admirable press release.

The truth is press releases are very formulaic. Because journalists expect facts and abhor unnecessarily complex language, a solid press release can be written by anyone as long as the writer follows the rules and has the release reviewed for obvious errors. Sure, it can take a little practice to get used to it, but there's no reason why anyone shouldn't be able to sit down and write a truly admirable press release.

And if you don't believe that, take this little tidbit right out of the horse's mouth: Most customers who purchase eReleases' professional writing services realize, after a few press releases, that it really isn't that difficult and they start writing their own highly effective, professional-grade press releases. That's bankable improvement, and eReleases wouldn't have it any other way. After all, who knows your business better than you do? You are your own best PR weapon.

That said, it can never hurt to brush up on some fundamentals. Don't think of this chapter as a collection of proprietary knowledge or insider information; it's stuff that you already know. We're just framing it in a way that specifically applies to press releases in order to dust off a few cobwebs. This way, you can sit down and write a press release with confidence in the abilities that you already have.

Where to Start?

Getting started is often the most difficult part of the process for those just beginning their PR efforts. The answer to where to start is simple, of course: Start off with information that is newsworthy. After all, it is a press release and you are sending it to media people in the hope that they turn it into a news story, so the best place to start is with something that is newsworthy.

This may come across as a task that is easier said than done, but it really isn't. Many people get themselves worked up about what is and isn't newsworthy because they think that only big stories are newsworthy when the opposite is much more true. Small stories are those that fill in the gap between the big stories, and people have to keep up with them just as much to stay informed. They take up more collective space than the big stories and they are much easier to process. Big or small, it's content either way, and becoming content is the ultimate goal of any press release.

So what are some typical newsworthy items that small businesses write press releases about? Just to name a few:

- new or updated product or service

- new or redesigned website

- personnel change: retirement, new hire, resignation, or death

- a sales promotion or special offer

- expert opinion on a subject within an industry

- winning an award/being singled out for an accomplishment

There are dozens of newsworthy reasons why a business should write a press release (for a longer list, see PR Fuel: http://tinyurl.com/Newsworthy-Ideas). Although the topics sometimes seem small, they are the events that keep the press and your industry aware of your company's activities. That is an essential part of a well-rounded media relationship. The more times you touch the media with a new press release, the easier it becomes, over time, to entice the media to cover your company.

Stay Focused

A press release should not be a hodgepodge of information. If there are a lot of events or developments happening at once, and you want people to know about all of them, great, you have multiple topics for multiple press releases. Don't just shove a whole bunch of information into one press release and be done with it. Even if it seems like that might be an effective cost-cutting measure, it can severely hurt you in the long term. Doing that not only muddles the message of a press release, making journalists less likely to use any of the information, it completely eliminates the opportunity to have your company's name in front of the press as often as possible. What are you more likely to remember — the name of a company that put out only one large release that you didn't even read fully, or the name of a company that is putting out a release a week that clearly and succinctly describe each of the improvements or advancements they are making?

Keeping press releases focused to one topic ensures that everything that has to be covered about the topic gets written. And without multiple issues or diversions, it also keeps them easy to read.

Before Sending a Press Release

Ask yourself the following before finalizing a press release:

- ✓ Has the information been shared in a way that is easy for journalists to use and for readers to understand?
- ✓ Has everything been summarized in a way that is concise and addresses all aspects of the information in a press release?
- ✓ Have you made sure the information is not false, libelous, or likely to cause unnecessary panic?
- ✓ Have you looked for opportunities to tighten the language and better balance excitement and boredom?

Have You Got a Story to Tell!

Creating a press release is about storytelling. If you think about it, everything boils down to sharing a narrative to keep the reader or listener captivated: relating the story of what you did earlier in the day with a friend or spouse, the plot of a blockbuster movie, a news story that everyone is talking about, etc.

For many press releases, the problem isn't that those sending them don't have important information to share, but rather that they don't know how to explain why their information is important. A newspaper editor once stated it best with a story of a public relations professional who never seemed to grasp the need to highlight important information in a press release:

Explain why the information is important.

"For years, we received press releases from a spokesperson of a major corporation. How he stayed in public relations for so long is something I never understood, because it seemed that the releases never got to the point. The releases he sent us were like someone telling a joke who either got the set-up wrong or couldn't remember the punchline. To add insult to injury, it seemed like he consistently got details wrong when it came to financial issues, dates, and the spelling of names.

"The result was that we gave little attention to any information that he sent us. We got our information from other sources if the release concerned an issue already in the news and pretty much ignored his press releases altogether."

The editor's story shares the sad reality that many people never grasp what is needed for an effective, compelling press release. It's assumed that the information the public relations professional shared was important, but he was totally clueless about how to bring out the importance of his topics and ensure that those details are accurate.

Be Captivating

The keys to being captivating in a press release are a keen focus on your subject and a thorough explanation of the subject's importance and consequence.

In fiction there are numerous stylistic actions that can be used to make a story compelling, but press releases are not works of fiction. The best way to create a compelling press release is to present information that people want to read. Just like the dilemma with writing about newsworthy topics, this sounds like it is easier said than done, but it really isn't.

Present information that people want to read.

When journalists read press releases containing business news, they are asking questions such as: "How can this information benefit my readers?"; "What kind of impact will this have on the industry?"; "Is this feature-worthy?"; and "Does this fit into my priorities as a well-informed journalist who wants to be ahead of the curve?"

These questions should look very familiar by now because they are nothing more than the 5 Ws.

This goes to show why the 5 Ws are absolutely necessary for any press release: They serve so many functions and add tremendous benefits to any release. They keep both writers and readers focused on their subject, they bring out all the newsworthy aspects in a release, and they communicate to the journalists who read them why a release contains valuable information.

The best way to focus on a topic, address all of its newsworthy aspects, fully understand the information's importance, and maximize its marketability toward journalists — all of the things that really make an effective press release — is to sit down and write out the 5 Ws of the topic.

Ask yourself what the 5 Ws of your release are: "Why is this something that I want everyone to know about?" or "How will this benefit people? How will it benefit us?" Delving further into your analysis might bring up considerations such as "I want to reach ... with this information," "This is important to my industry because ...," "This information needs to go out now so that ...." After thinking about and writing down these questions and considerations, you will not only be focused on the topic at hand; you will also have an outline of important information.

When we talked about the 5 Ws earlier, we used an analogy of them being like the ingredients needed for a recipe. For someone writing a

Assemble thoughts in a style that piques excitement and curiosity.

press release, whether it's a novice or veteran public relations practitioner, defining the 5 Ws of your press release is akin to making a list of needed ingredients and taking the time to purchase them.

The following pages examine how the essentials of your press release can be woven together to create information that is to the point, factual, and exciting. Anyone can write down their thoughts and call the result a press release. The pros, however, know how to assemble their thoughts in a style that piques excitement and curiosity.

Let's take a look at the process every press release has to pass through to assure that it's compelling:

1. Begin by asking whether the information in the press release has any value to the public and why. Address this issue by reviewing the 5 Ws.

2. Next, make sure that the information is organized in a fashion that makes it easy to understand. Specifically, don't overload press releases with too much information. Staying focused helps with this. Don't be negative. A press release with a negative tone is like a party guest who is always whining — he doesn't realize how fortunate he is to be in good company, and he won't be invited back. Plus, negativity is a distraction from the purpose of a release. Finally, does one point easily lead to another?

3. Then ask yourself whether the information in your press release is captivating. The best way to make a release captivating is to review why the information is important and consequential. Interesting facts are strong motivators. One thing that can help add to a captivating release is to add a call to action. After reviewing a topic's importance, give readers an outlet by telling them what they can do with their new information. This can be anything from "For more information, visit the following website" to "Interested parties may sign up now at …."

4. Finally, is the information in your press release timely? Timing can mean everything when it comes to issuing a release. It makes little sense to release a statement about a news item a week after it has occurred and the media have already moved on to covering other stories. Likewise, issuing a press release too early — such as one about a Christmas event that goes out in the height of spring — can result in it being diverted for use later, meaning it runs the risk of being lost altogether.

How You Say It — Words and Grammar

"The shorter and plainer the better."

-Beatrix Potter, author of *The Tale of Peter Rabbit*

One of the reasons why people start off thinking that they can't write a press release on their own is because they just don't think that they are very good writers. They don't want to embarrass themselves because they can't think of impressive words that will razzle-dazzle people, or they can't string together complicated ideas in complex sentences.

When it comes to press releases, that's a good thing! There are few things that will get a release ignored more quickly than 10-cent words and sentences that are artfully vague.

The best press releases are written plainly and simply. They state the facts with as little fuss as possible and then stop. Because of this, there are a few things that are better left on the editing room floor, such as:

- adjectives – especially subjective ones like "exciting," "fabulous," or "revolutionary"

- adverbs – such as "really," "extremely" or "very"

- exclamation marks

- unsupported opinions

Keep adjectives and adverbs out of a press release.

Keeping these elements out of a press release will not only keep you in favor with journalists, it will make the release read better. Just take a look at the following example, which reads like an unfortunate number of press releases:

Because of its amazing speed and unbelievable affordability, the SuperChip 3000 is quickly becoming the industry standard for processors, easily leaving the competition in the dust!

Though this may seem like an exaggeration, it is close to what journalists have to sift through countless times a day. This is what causes them to ignore a majority of the press releases they receive. The ironic thing is that the information hidden in the previous example is great information that most technology journalists would be glad to cover. This next example shows the same claim, written in a more appropriate manner, that would likely win the attention of journalists:

Because of its speed and affordability, the SuperChip 3000 is becoming the industry standard for processors.

From that sentence, a press release would likely move on to discuss how the product's speed and price compare to the competition, then maybe cite some sales statistics showing how quickly the processor is being adopted by the industry.

Guidelines for Solid Press Release Style

In sticking with the theme of keeping things simple, it should come as no surprise that sticking to the basics of writing and grammar is the golden rule for press release writing. Here is a quick refresher course on some writing basics that should be employed.

The Third Person

Writing in the third person is the first and best guideline to writing a press release with the proper tone. Grammatically, third person refers to people or objects using the pronouns "he," "she," "it," or "they." It creates the distance of an outsider looking in, instead of the "I" or "you" of first and second person, respectively. All newspapers write in the third person because it is the only way to write objectively, without introducing personal feelings or opinions.

Write in the third person, with "he," "she," "it," or "they."

When writing a press release, think of it like a story that you would read in a newspaper. Articles you read in the news are never written like conversations; they never start off like, "I was talking to John the other day," or "You have probably never seen something like this before," and that's because newspapers try to maintain a professional distance.

If you are having trouble staying in the third person while you write, it can help to think about how the points you want to say would be written in a newspaper. Even though you aren't writing a newspaper article, writing a release that sounds like one is an easy way to stay in the right person. Consider these examples:

- Instead of writing "You can benefit from ...," use "Consumers can benefit ...," or something more precise like, "Holiday shoppers can benefit ...."

- Rather than writing, "We have been operating for more than 20 years," write, "Gregson Pharmaceuticals has been operating for more than 20 years."

Reserve "I" and "we" for direct quotes from experts and company principals.

Action Verbs

Verbs are words that denote an action or a state of being in a sentence, but not all verbs are created equal. Grammatically, action verbs are just verbs that convey action, as opposed to auxiliary verbs like "to be," but there are action verbs, and there are *action* verbs, which are more vivid than other verbs. Instead of saying "run," an action equivalent would be "sprint," while "look into" can became "examine" or "research," and so on.

Action verbs serve a valuable purpose.

Action verbs are the one area where you can be a bit flashy with your writing, but they serve a valuable purpose. Action verbs help to engage the reader, as well as convey ideas more concisely. But they can be overused, so be careful how you use them. Also, if you have a hard time trying to think of some good action verbs, keep in mind that writing plainly is still key, and if you can do that without action verbs, then you are still doing fine.

This first sentence is OK, but relatively humdrum:

This year's sales figures doubled those from the year before, and were above analysts' expectations, making XYZ Corp.'s position as an industry leader certain.

But it can easily be jazzed up with two action verbs:

This year's sales figures doubled those from the year before, shattering analysts' expectations and solidifying XYZ Corp.'s position as an industry leader.

Subject-Verb Agreement

Without getting very technical, a subject is what a sentence is about, and every complete sentence has one. (*She* is a great chef. *These pretzels* are making me thirsty.) Every subject consists of a noun or noun phrase.

Nouns can be either singular or plural (e.g., dog, dogs; computer, computers). Verbs, too, can be either singular or plural (e.g., is, are; buys, buy). Since there is essentially going to be a noun and a verb in every sentence, it is in everyone's best interests to make sure that they get along. Subject-Verb agreement simply means that when you have a plural subject, you should have a plural verb, and vice-versa for singulars.

Anaheim Electronics [singular], according to a recent report by the AEUG, sells[singular] more diodes than any other electronics company. The report shows that even combined, all other companies[plural] sell [plural] only half as much as Anaheim.

For any further clarification on subject-verb agreement, as well as examples of its nuances, visit the Purdue University Online Writing Lab at http://tinyurl.com/subject-verb.

Consistent Verb Tense

In English, we use verb tenses to delineate events that occurred in the past and events that are happening now. Keeping these tenses straight is an important consideration for a press release. Unlike subject-verb agreement, where you try to get two things to agree within a sentence, verb tense should be used consistently throughout an entire document. Switching tenses is considered to be highly amateur.

When writing a press release, you may use past, present or future tense as long as you do so uniformly. There is, though, a guideline for which tense to use depending on the nature of the release. In general, hard news stories typically use the past tense, while soft news stories use the present. Hard news typically consists of facts, figures, and important business information (e.g., announcing a merger, sales figures, current events). It is basically "serious" news. Soft news can be related to entertainment, human interest, and lifestyle, among others. When talking about an event that has not yet taken place, you would use future tense.

You may use past, present or future tense as long as you do so uniformly.

Enfield Tennis, LLC announced today the promotion of Hal Incandenza to the position of CEO. The long-term COO was unanimously voted in by the board of directors after a brief discussion. (past tense/hard news)

In James Caulfield's new novel, 'School Days,' readers are taken though the life and times of a 1930s Harvard student who can't quite find his direction in life. (present tense/soft news)

Salad Days, a family-friendly restaurant in North Sundance, will be hosting Carl the Clown next Saturday at 1:30 p.m. in a performance that will be free for any family with a child under age five. (future tense/upcoming event)

For any further clarification on tense consistency, as well as hints on how to control shifts in tense, visit the Purdue University Online Writing Lab at http://tinyurl.com/tense-consistency.

Active Voice

Active and passive voice have to do with whether or not the subject of a sentence is performing or receiving the action of the verb. If the subject of a sentence is performing the action, then the sentence is active. If the subject is receiving the action, then it is passive.

A typical example of the active voice would be "Jessica hit the ball." That sentence is active because Jessica is the subject of the sentence and she is the one performing the action. This sentence is about Jessica, so she's the subject, and she is actively doing something, so the sentence is active.

That same sentence in the passive voice would read, "The ball was hit by Jessica." That sentence is about the ball, so the ball is the subject, but it is receiving the action, rather than doing it, so it's passive.

Writing experts advise the use of active voice for most writing situations, and press releases are no exception. Typically, it's best to use the active voice because it promotes a sense of immediacy and gets readers more involved with what is written. The passive voice tends to hide important information at the end of a sentence. Jessica is the one doing the action; she is what readers want to read about. Yet in the passive version of the sentence, you don't find out about her until the end of the sentence, and the ball, which no one really cares about, is featured prominently.

Use the active voice in press releases.

So with your sentences, as with your press releases, make sure you state your important information right away and get to the less important details later. Here are a few examples to put this in a more PR context:

- Instead of "The new technology was created by Mendelson Labs," write, "Mendelson Labs created the new technology."

- Instead of "In the new legislation by Congresswoman Jennifer Walters," put, "In Congresswoman Jennifer Walters' new legislation."

For any further clarification on the active and passive voices, as well as how to transform one into the other, visit the Purdue University Online Writing Lab at http://tinyurl.com/active-passive-voice.

Use the Inverted Triangle

The most basic style of writing that should be taken to heart by anyone attempting to write press releases is called the "inverted triangle." It is easily the most practical way of conveying written information and is used extensively by journalists. By writing in this style you conform to journalists' expectations and heighten your chances of your release getting read more thoroughly.

The inverted triangle shares the most important information in a story first, followed by additional details that support and further explain the main information. As a release goes on, the information shared becomes less and less essential. When you use the inverted triangle, journalists can understand the substance of a story even if they read only the headline and a few paragraphs, if that much. This is a big help when some journalists are trying to go through hundreds of press releases a day. The following graphic shows how releases written in the style of the inverted triangle should be constructed.

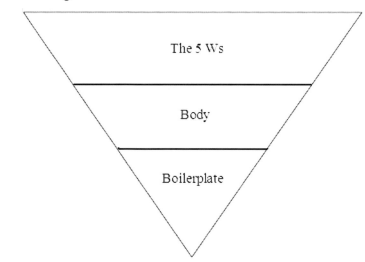

The origins of the inverted triangle are varied, but most credit its beginnings to the Civil War. Many suggest it was created in response to the invention of the telegraph, with reporters encouraged to share the most important details of a story first in case telegraph lines dropped out or were cut. It was preferable for reporters to transmit their complete stories, but it was crucial for them to convey their key points first.

The inverted triangle is important for a press release because:

- Like a news story, it immediately lets journalists know what is important about your release, as opposed to making them search for its substance.

- It helps busy reporters quickly determine why they should cover your information and makes it convenient for them to pitch the story to their editors.

- The more that a press release is written in an inverted triangle style, the easier it is to translate it into a news story and, consequently, the chances are greater that it will be used.

Let's take a look at the first few paragraphs of a press release that doesn't use an inverted triangle style, followed by one that does:

A local manufacturer expressed excitement this week about the development of several new products.

"I'm excited about what we're doing with our new products and believe the community will find them to be invaluable," said Bob Walsh.

Walsh is CEO of Housewares Limited, a locally owned producer of housewares. He said the new products will be available for purchase as Christmas gifts.

The products include cooking utensils, serving trays, table centerpieces, specialty coffees, and other items. The products should be ready for purchase November 8.

"These items are not only ideal for holiday entertaining, but will also make perfect gifts," Walsh said.

The problem with the example above is that all of the 5 Ws are addressed, but the release buries them in the body of the text.

On the other hand, a release that uses an inverted triangle structure might begin like this:

Housewares Limited announced today the release of several products in time for the holiday season that are perfect both as Christmas gifts and for seasonal parties.

Bob Walsh, chairman of the locally owned manufacturer, said the new products include cooking utensils, serving trays, table centerpieces, specialty coffees, and other items that will be available for purchase beginning November 8.

Don't bury the 5 Ws deep in the text.

"I'm excited about what we're doing with our new products and believe the community will find them to be invaluable," Walsh said. "These items are not only ideal for holiday entertaining, but will also be the right gift for someone special."

The second example shares the 5 Ws almost immediately so that readers will know what products are available, when they can be purchased, and who can benefit from them. Not only does the second example include the important information at the top of the release; it also includes the same information by using fewer words and summarizing them in a concise manner.

Once you've written a release that's informative, exciting, and puts the most important information first, you're pretty much home free, right? Well, almost. First, there are a few other matters to consider.

Remember, It's a Press Release — Not Ad Copy

A press release that sounds too much like ad copy can be fatal, even when you're attempting to create excitement about a product you're hoping to sell. The reason is simple: Reporters and editors want to know why the information in your release is important to their readers — but have little interest in helping you benefit from the information. Consumers reading the release want to know why they should purchase your product but don't have any interest in reading a release that is overbearing. A release that reads like sales copy and sounds too good to be true is like a pesky salesperson, and can most people honestly say they would sit down and listen to a pushy sales pitch if they had the option not to? Save the ad copy for actual advertising.

Issuing a press release that reads more like an advertisement than like a news story not only runs a risk of being ignored (a near certainty), it's an easy way for an organization to damage its credibility. And the more it happens, the more it will diminish the media's interest in using anything the organization submits in the future.

Newswires have strict rules against press releases that read too much like sales copy.

Also, keep in mind that newswires have strict rules against press releases that read too much like sales copy. Wires will flatly reject any release that too closely resembles an advertisement. So it's best to avoid writing like that entirely.

To make sure a press release doesn't read like ad copy, remember these suggestions:

- Unless it is used in a quote, do not use "you" in a press release.

- Limit the use of adjectives and adverbs as much as possible.

- Absolutely no exclamation points should be used ... unless your company's name is Yahoo!

- Avoid outlandish claims that make the information in your release sound too good to be true. If any claim really is that incredible, make sure you back it up with metrics, data, or other objective measures.

- Stay away from attacks on competing products. This is a turnoff for most people because it shows that the only way you can hawk your product is through tearing down the competition.

- Avoid leading with price or discounts in your headline

and opening paragraph. The media does not promote deals or special discounts unless they approach the absurd like a $1 laptop or $1,500 hamburger. In fact, the media makes a practice of avoiding the absurd as most are designed to create buzz and are always accompanied with strings and limitations as in the case of the $1 laptop (a limit of three at this price).

- In addition, the media turns a skeptical eye towards promotions and contests because of abusive behavior and scams on the Internet. You have to be a recognized brand with a strong reputation to get sizeable media attention if you plan on holding a contest or giveaway.

- Don't use different sized fonts, font styles, garish colors, or any other formatting styles associated with advertising copy.

Proofread

Proofreading is an essential part of any writing process, but it is often overlooked, leading to unintended consequences. Everyone who writes a press release should proofread it multiple times before sending it to journalists and the newswire. This should be a given, but in case there are still those who need to be convinced, consider these ramifications:

- Grammatical errors not only make your text difficult to read, they can also make your message difficult to understand, especially when you accidentally omit words.

- Spelling errors are considered to be the height of unprofessionalism. Many journalists consider press releases with spelling errors to be disrespectful or even insulting. Why should they waste their time looking over something that someone doesn't even care enough about to spell-check?

- Misspelled names can result in inaccurate reporting. When there are inconsistencies in names or facts, chances are that rather than taking the time to research the right information, busy media outlets will disregard the information altogether.

- Mistakes about times and dates, monetary figures, and other information can lead to confusion. The media can't report the facts of your press release correctly if you've provided them with information that is erroneous.

- Mistakes in a press release reduce your credibility. Everyone's human, so small mistakes are forgivable, but constant or big mistakes just waste a reporter's time. The more it happens, or even if it's one egregious error, the more likely it is that journalists will ignore future press releases entirely.

Almost always, after spending a lot of time trying to craft a press release perfectly, a writer will simply be too close to the information to see any faults. The mind has a way of inserting what you meant to say on the page, rather than seeing what's actually on it. To keep those mistakes from being released, here are a few suggestions for effective proofreading:

- **Print your release.** There is something about a computer screen that makes certain mistakes hard to catch, so print your release when you feel you have a final draft. The different medium may help make mistakes easier to spot.

- **Use a red pen.** Red pens are good for editing and corrections because they make the corrections stand out. When proofing, mark all the errors that you see and be specific about how to correct them. It's too easy to forget what that circle or abbreviated note meant; if you are specific, you bypass that problem.

- **Read the release out loud.** If it doesn't read well out loud, it won't read well on the page. When you read a piece of writing aloud, it's easy to tell when a sentence runs on or is confusingly written because it will leave you tongue-tied, stammering or just plain weary.

- **Ask two or three other people to read your work.** The more unfamiliar they are with the information in the press release the better, but that's not always possible. Have them mark down any problems they see.

- **Do it again.** Each time you enter corrections and think you have a final draft, print a new copy and proofread again. Sometimes you won't find anything wrong, but more often than not, something slipped through that was staring you in the face the whole time.

If you prefer an alternative to the hard-copy approach, then make sure to write your press releases using software that allows the insertion of editorial comments and tracks changes and corrections. Most word processors, including Microsoft Word, have these functions available.

Newswire Standards

While a newswire may have some strict standards about what it will and will not run, these standards are all born of good causes. And since running a press release over a newswire is the single best way to put that release in front of as many journalists as possible, it is in everyone's best interest to follow the guidelines. Here is a list of a few things that will stop any release from being sent over a Tier 1 wire:

Follow newswire guidelines for acceptable content.

- **References to celebrities.** Mentioning a celebrity in any way can be seen as that celebrity endorsing your product or company. Even if a celebrity is seen using your product every day or has praised your product in person or in writing, unless that celebrity is a contracted endorser of your company, he or she should not be mentioned. Every celebrity has a team of lawyers looking for ways to justify their salaries, so any unapproved mention of a celebrity can land your company and the newswire in a legal quagmire.

- **Nudity.** Obviously pictures of nudity can't be in the text of a release. Yet you should still make sure that any links to websites that are included in the press release or any pictures that will be distributed along with the release are not explicit. That is not to say that everything sexually oriented is prohibited; releases about adult products, strip clubs, etc. are issued regularly. It's just that a release itself can't be explicit. Links within a press release should not lead to content that is above a PG rating.

- **Advertisements.** We've already mentioned that newswires won't allow press releases that read too much like advertisements.

- **Stock ticker symbols.** This is a bit different in that it's not that it absolutely isn't allowed, it's just highly scrutinized. PR Newswire, for example, has a page-long policy on when it will and will not allow stock ticker symbols. It's worth noting also that if a company is public, it has to deal directly with the newswire, not with money-saving third-party partners like eReleases. Public companies have to live with higher standards because the news they release can affect significant sums of money.

- **Defamation.** Newswires usually refuse to distribute any material that could be construed as libelous, slanderous or unfairly damaging to the reputation of a person or company. Thus you need to be careful what you say about specific competitors or specific products in a press release.

Chapter 4

Press Release Style and Formatting

Pleasing the Editors

When it comes to press releases, style is important — both as it relates to editorial content and to format. Issue a release that neglects some of the editorial considerations that were just discussed, and the information will be difficult to understand. This means that your hope that a press release will be turned into an article or a story likely won't be realized. The same applies to format, which assures that a press release looks like a press release.

Your style must be consistent and effective.

Let's start by examining how style is important when it comes to editorial content. To assure that a press release adequately conveys its message, the style has to be consistent and effective. Among the key points to remember are:

1. **Font style**. Font styles and sizes really aren't an issue since the wire will convert text into its standard format. Keep that in mind when writing anything with any kind of formatting because newswires have a limited ability to transmit typography. Some newswires support boldface, italics, and bullet points, but that doesn't mean every site or outlet that picks up the release will honor that formatting.

2. **Quotes**. Use quotation marks around statements when they are comments made by someone. Quotes should be kept to a high standard and be used only when they are of particular importance to the information in the release. Quotes should state something that is so great or precisely worded that the media would be doing a disservice to paraphrase the message. Most quotes fail this test and will not be included in any articles or stories developed from the press release.

3. **Say it, don't scream it**. Capitalize words or acronyms that are usually uppercased (e.g., NASA), but stay away from capitalizing for emphasis. This makes a press release hard to read, and its impact is like someone who is screaming. Also avoid capitalizing words that are not usually in uppercase and capitalizing certain words randomly throughout the release. Normally, the only items that should be in all-caps are "FOR IMMEDIATE RELEASE" at the

very top of the page, the city in the dateline, and acronyms.

> BE SURE THAT THE INFORMATION IN YOUR PRESS RELEASE IS IMPORTANT!!! YOU CAN CONVEY THAT BY HOW YOU WRITE YOUR RELEASE, RATHER THAN USING ALL UPPERCASED LETTERS, WHICH IS HARD TO READ AND ANNOYING.

4. **Where's the beef?** Most releases run from 350 to 500 words from start to finish. That means everything from the headline down to the last letter of the contact information. Any text beyond that runs the risk of wasting precious newswire real estate.

Knowing the Rules

Just as a press release must adhere to a certain editorial style to be taken seriously by editors, its formatted appearance also has a hand to play in its overall effectiveness.

Many of the individual elements of press releases have their own stylistic guidelines that give releases a uniform appearance. They include:

1. **FOR IMMEDIATE RELEASE.** This is the first thing that should be on any press release. It goes on the very top of the page and should be written in all caps. It announces that a press-ready news lead is there for the taking.

2. **The Headline.** Headlines should be only about one line long (60-80 characters). Sometimes a second line is needed, but usually anything longer than a line that isn't immediately required for the core of the message should be relegated to a subhead. Limit yourself to only one succinct subhead.

   Headlines should be written as if they were the title of a book or article, with all of the important words capitalized. There are many specific guidelines on what should and shouldn't be capitalized in a headline, but they don't all agree. Common wisdom on title-casing dictates capitalization of all words except articles and prepositions. Prepositions of four characters or more are sometimes uppercase; newswires are generally flexible about this. For subheads, capitalize only the first word and any proper nouns.

   Also, any internal punctuation is fine, like commas or semicolons, but end punctuation (i.e., periods, exclamation points) is not necessary in the headline unless it's a question. (But do try to avoid using a question as a headline or subhead. It detracts from positioning yourself as authority, even when the question is rhetorical. You are the one with the answers, not the questions, after all. Simply put, make a statement.)

When it comes to a subhead, rules tend to go out the window with current practice by PR practitioners. Some subheads are written in title case with no end punctuation while other subheads are written in sentence style with no special capitalization other than would be used in a normal sentence. End punctuation is fine to include at the end of the subhead if you are using the sentence style but not if you are using the title case approach. Consistency is the key.

3. **Dateline.** The dateline of a press release immediately precedes the beginning of the first paragraph. It shares the location of a release's origins as well as the date that it was released over the wire. The city is always capitalized, while the state is abbreviated according to AP style — not US Postal Code style. Since AP style formatting is best, acquire a copy of the Associated Press style handbook and let it be your guide. Its formal title is The Associated Press Stylebook and Briefing on Media Law, and a new edition generally comes out every year or two. It's available at most online bookstores or from http://www.ap.org/. Do note that according to AP guidelines, some city names stand alone and don't require a state listing. If you use a press release service like eReleases, there's no need to sweat the small stuff like proper format of your dateline because each press release receives two levels of editorial review.

With a press release service like eReleases, each press release receives two levels of editorial review.

The date listed on the release after the city/state is the actual date the release is distributed.

HUNTSVILLE, Ala., Sept. 14, 2005 — The City of Huntsville announced on Monday spending cuts to the department of public safety that will impact the city's 234,000 residents in the areas of police protection, fire and rescue, and 911 operations.

Where this press release said "Monday," it could also have said "today." Using either is acceptable in a release.

4. **Boilerplate.** Boilerplate copy can be used to provide recipients of a release with additional information about a company or organization. This is the final opportunity to define why the company issuing the release brings something to the table. Though it is recommended, it is an optional element, particularly in instances when a company needs to sacrifice that language to accommodate vital information directly related to the purpose of

the release and ensure that a release does not become too lengthy.

Boilerplate should be preceded by a heading that says "About Company," but, of course, replace the word "Company" with the name of your company.

About Deep Web Technologies

Deep Web Technologies (http://www.deepwebtech.com) creates custom, sophisticated federated search solutions for clients who demand precise, accurate results. The tool of choice when needing to access the deep web, federated search performs real-time, parallel searches of multiple information sources, merging the results into one page. Serving Fortune 500 companies, the Science.gov Alliance (http://www.science.gov), the U.S. Dept. of Energy, the Dept. of Defense, Scitopia.org (http://www.scitopia.org), Nutrition.gov, WorldWideScience.org (http://www.worldwidescience.org) and a variety of other customers and partners, Deep Web Technologies has built a reputation as the "researcher's choice" for its advanced, agile information discovery tools.

---

5. **Contact Information.** Contact information should be the last thing in a press release. Ideally, contact information should include a name, that person's title, phone number, e-mail address, and the company's website. But don't write them out so that they end up as one long line. Give each separate bit of information its own line so that it is all easy to see and journalists don't have to go hunting for the information. A physical street address or mailing address is neither needed nor recommended.

Give each bit of contact information its own line.

Keep in mind that press contact information is generally public information. There is an option at most newswires to designate the information as "media only," but the technology of newswire operations is such that the full release information can leak through and become public copy via some of the news feeds that carry newswire content. Therefore, a business line is always preferable to a home or mobile number.

If you're concerned about your contact information for the media becoming public, there are services that can create a temporary phone number with voicemail and/or forwarding service for less than $10 a month. In the case of e-mail addresses, some newswires try to cloak e-mail addresses so they will be less susceptible to phishing, or being used for non-media purposes such as contacting you with a sales pitch or flooding your inbox with spam. However, it's essential that you be responsive to an e-mail from a reporter, editor or producer who read your press release, so if you create a special e-mail address for press releases you must be sure to monitor it closely.

Contact:

First and Last Name

Director of Operations

555-555-5555

name@website.com

http://www.website.com

6. **Are you finished?** Though it is more a practice of tradition now, press releases normally have a clear indication that the release is finished.

   Regardless of whether the release is several pages long or even just a few paragraphs, signify the end of the release by centering either -30- or # # # below the last paragraph as shown below:

   The company said that it hopes to have services restored to customers to minimize any inconvenience that may be created by the power outage.

   # # #

   Though the exact origins aren't fully known, it is said that telegraph operators ended telegraph transmissions with "XXX" to indicate when a transmission was finished. This eventually morphed into -30-, a numeric translation of the Roman numerals XXX. While the -30- is still used today, it is more common to use "# # #" to end a press release.

If It Quacks Like a Press Release

Not only do the elements of a press release have a standard style and format, so too does the release in its entirety. The following is a template that shows the standard formatting that a release should follow:

FOR IMMEDATE RELEASE

Headline

Optional Subhead

CITY, State, Month XX, 20XX — Opening Paragraph

Body Paragraphs (3-5)

Optional Boilerplate

Contact:

Name of Media Contact

Title of Media Contact

Company Name

Contact Phone Number

Contact E-mail

Website URL

# # #

There is quite a bit of white space in the formatting, but it is there so that the text will be easier to read on a computer screen, which is how most, if not all, journalists will see a release.

To further illustrate how to use this template, as well as review the style tips that we have gone over, see the following instructional sample:

FOR IMMEDIATE RELEASE

Headlines Should Explain the Basis for the Release in One Sentence

Subheads are optional and should include pertinent information that can't fit or doesn't need to be in the headline

CITY, State [follow AP Style abbreviations], Month [abbreviated if more than five letters] Day, Year — This opening paragraph is where you should write a concise overview of the most important information in your release. Present the 5 Ws. These first couple of sentences should be straight to the point.

After the opening paragraph, the following paragraphs should more fully explain the purpose of the release. Make sure to stay topical and informative so that journalists will keep reading. You can easily do this by addressing the five basic questions that journalists are concerned with: who, what, when, where, and why. Be concise and pithy; aim for 350-500 words total for the entire release.

"Quotes shouldn't be used often — one is best — and they should contain worthwhile information that comes from someone prominent or important in the company," said John Doe, founder of YourCompany, LLC. Use the person's full name the first time you mention him or her.

"If you have to quote or refer to someone more than once, just use his or her last name each subsequent time," said Doe.

Don't forget to write out the address of your website fully, like this: http://www.likethis.com. Don't worry about that last period; it won't break or invalidate the link. If you want to include your website's URL mid-sentence as a modifier rather than as a subject or object, then put parenthesis around it (http://www.likethis.com).

For more information, visit http://www.yourwebsite.com or call John Doe at (555) 555-5555.

About YourCompany, LLC

This is where you can put a boilerplate. A boilerplate is a short paragraph that explains the identity of a company and what it does. Boilerplate is optional, but it doesn't hurt to have one to help identify your business. Think of boilerplates as a thumbnail sketch of your company that provides a little background information to the press.

Contact:

John Doe

Founder

YourCompany, LLC

555-555-5555

JohnDoe@website.com

http://www.website.com

# # #

Keeping Up With the Associated Press

When writing becomes something that you focus on and do, rather than just something that comes up when you have to send an e-mail, a multitude of small, pesky questions can stump you. Does this have to be hyphenated? What's the established way of saying this? Can I abbreviate a word this way?

The answers to these questions and more are found in style books. There are a number of different style books out there, all with their own take on such questions, but since press releases are distributed to journalists and media outlets, using the Associated Press (AP) style is the correct choice.

The Associated Press Stylebook and Briefing on Media Law addresses a variety of issues, including the spelling of certain words, preferred state abbreviations, how to denote formal titles and ranks, and dozens of other tips. It is a nearly essential reference in making sure that a press release is written in proper journalistic style. Often referred to by the shorter title, *The AP Stylebook*, it's a bible to journalists and anyone serious about writing press releases.

So if press releases are going to become a cornerstone in your public relations strategy — and they should — then picking up a copy is a good idea. If you prefer, you can purchase an online subscription to it at http://www.apstylebook.com/. Along with allowing access to information from any desktop and real-time updates, the online version enables companies to customize the manual to individual style issues relevant specifically to them.

Chapter 5

Determining and Appealing to Your Audience

Do You Really Know the Ideal Recipient of Your Information?

So far, we've discussed the elements of putting together a winning press release, but that is only part of the equation. Make no mistake, failing to identify your proper audience can put your message in the wrong hands at the wrong time. Avoiding such a scenario begins by asking the following questions:

1. What is your demographic and are you targeting it?

2. Is there a need for the product or service you are marketing? If so, are you releasing information that lets consumers know that? Have you effectively shared the news if there have been improvements to the products or services you provide?

3. Is the angle of your press release designed to engage and hook the media's interest?

4. Are you directing your press release to the right reporter/editor within a media organization — one who covers information for your target demographic?

When it comes to press releases, achieving the coverage and response you want also involves knowing where to pitch the products you are promoting. An eReleases client who wanted to get the biggest bang for his buck saw that our Business industry list was quite large, as well as our Advertising/Marketing industry list. The problem was that his product was a woman's fashion accessory. He was advised against sending the press release to these two off-target industry lists and to choose relevant media, such as those in Women's Interests and Fashion. He attempted to justify his idea by arguing that businessmen and executives might buy the accessory for their wives, ignoring the question: What business or ad/marketing journalist would write about such a product?

Have your release sent to the appropriate audience.

In the end, the client decided to take the chance and received almost no media attention. When he finally conceded that his way might have been misguided, he paid to have the press release distributed to the proper media, gaining mentions in customer-oriented magazines and fashion trade publications, as well as blogs, websites, and a podcast. It is better to reach 100 targeted media than to send your press release to 10,000 off-target media.

Who Is My Audience?

Press releases have at lease two audiences: one that is unique to an individual release, and one that is shared by all releases. The audience for which every press release is written is, as noted earlier, journalists.

We have already established that press releases are not articles; they don't normally get published in newspapers, and they aren't run over the AP newswire. Although they become accessible to anyone when posted online, press releases are primarily for journalists, so they have to appeal to journalists. They are the ones who will potentially write stories about your press release, but they don't just do that for any company or any single bit of information. This is why having a robust relationship with the media is so important.

Building Relationships with the Media

"If you don't do your research and if you don't take your time, you're not going to get the job done. The people who give the PR industry a bad name are the people who don't realize or accept a simple fact: We control the information, but the media brings it to the public. Don't antagonize the media, but don't kiss their ass. There's a happy medium and you get there by learning, researching and studying. And if you're not willing to do that, then you're not going to be in this business long." - Anonymous PR Firm Vice President

Building up relationships with the media is a long and involved process. Like any relationship, media relationships require work, but the more they are worked on, the more mutually beneficial they become and the happier everyone is in the long run. Though some of the points to remember go beyond press releases themselves, there are a few key things to keep in mind for a good media relationship.

- Never put a journalist on the spot. Interactions should always be light, cordial and unobtrusive.

- Never spam journalists, hoping that the right journalist will take your information and run with it.

- Know the needs of different media outlets in regard to the different types of stories they cover.

- Know and respect the media's deadlines to guarantee that you are not contacting them at the wrong time.

Being Involved in Your Industry

Often the first and best step toward having a strong relationship with the media, as well as your industry-specific audience, is to simply be involved. This sounds like a basic step, but many small business owners, though passionate about their field, seemingly don't feel the need to be involved with the more dedicated aspects of their industry.

Being involved means reading trade publications, local newspapers, blogs, and websites and attending trade shows. This is all-around good advice because it not only allows you to become more familiar with the journalists who cover your industry, it keeps you informed of what customers want and what competing companies are up to.

Research which reporter covers which beat.

While reading the newspaper and trade magazines, make note of who is writing what. When it comes to the newspaper, local or otherwise, journalists all cover a certain beat, so it doesn't do any good to try and talk to just anyone at a newspaper. Keep tabs on who is covering stories that are relevant to your business. Depending on what you do, there may be one or a dozen journalists covering stories on your industry.

Make sure to read what those who cover your industry write. It only does so much good to know that someone writes about your industry. To know how that journalist covers your industry's news is a whole other ballpark entirely.

Taking Those First Steps

There are two different kinds of relationships that can be developed with the media: those that you develop through frequent communications via a newswire, and those you foster personally.

In respect to the wire, relationships are forged through frequent, substantive press release communications. That's not to say you need to issue a press release every day, each with earth-shattering news. But one release can be easily missed. Or journalists, unfamiliar with a company, might take a "wait and see" approach. Any way it happens, the best approach to building a press relationship over the wire is to release information consistently and be as responsive as possible to any feedback.

It happens too frequently that someone, unsure of the necessity for press releases in his or her PR efforts, will hazard a chance and issue one press release then see what comes of it. When there is little or no response, the sender feels justified in his or her caution and decides not to issue press releases anymore.

This is categorically the wrong approach. On the wire, where hundreds of journalists have the ability to see your information, it is doubtful that you will be able to develop a personal business relationship with even a fraction of them. In this environment, where there are hundreds of journalists and an untold number of people vying for their attention, reputation and recognition take the place of a personal business relationship. So just releasing a single press release on the wire is a lot like saying "hi" to a stranger on the street one day and then wondering why the person doesn't call the next.

The more press releases a company issues, the more familiar that company becomes to journalists and the greater the archive the company has of their changes and deeds in the public record. How frequently a company should issue a press release really depends on the company. It all depends on how frequently newsworthy things happen for a company. Some companies have enough going on that they can put out releases weekly or even daily, but most small businesses achieve their best results with monthly releases. Quarterly is about as infrequent as any public relations effort can get while still maintaining a presence with the media.

Quarterly is the minimum frequency for issuing press releases.

Outside of the wire, relationship-building becomes more one-on-one and should be reserved for those select few local and trade journalists who immediately cover your industry. It takes a lot of time and effort to build up the kind of relationship that most PR professionals want with journalists, so having only a limited number of press contacts is advisable. Otherwise, maintaining those relationships will become too difficult, or some journalists will fall by the wayside.

After doing research on which journalists cover your kind of business, whether in the local newspapers, trade publications, or blogs, the best way to start a relationship is to approach them when you don't have a press release or anything you want from them in return. Like any other relationship in life, just introduce yourself and maybe make a comment about something that you thought was particularly insightful in one of their recent articles. Show them that you follow them and actually know a little about their body of work.

Business Casual

After introducing yourself to the journalists, make it a point to keep up with them: not in a pesky way, of course, but four or five times a year is good. Maybe you see an article somewhere that covers something interesting that you don't see a lot of people talking about? Feel free to forward information like that along in an e-mail and just mention how you thought he or she would find it interesting. Or maybe send a greeting card for an often-overlooked holiday. Chat with media contacts at trade shows. Try anything that would be memorable or set you apart from the pack without being sensational or obtrusive.

There is a line that shouldn't be crossed, though, and that's at doing things to try to get favors. Journalists have a strict ethical code so that they can remain unbiased and maintain their integrity. Anything that a PR person does to infringe on that code — such as giving gifts or swag — not only irreparably damages the relationship between the journalist and the company, but it could cost some people their jobs. So it's best to steer clear of that area completely and keep press relationships light, professional, and free. Review copies of products are typically the only exception to this rule, as well as the occasional meal if you are able to cultivate such a close relationship. Every journalist and media outlet has its own set of rules on how to define what is and is not ethical. It is imperative to learn, understand, and respect these rules for all of your media contacts.

Journalists have a strict ethical code.

If you have taken the time to build up a relationship with a handful of journalists, sending out a press release to them is very easy. Just e-mail it to them, maybe a few days before it goes to the wire, and tell them that you are just sending them a "heads up" on the release. That way they can have a little bit of exclusivity that will help build up your relations.

If there are multiple reporters that you know at a single publication that could cover your news, make sure to send it to all of them in a way that they know other people are receiving the same information. The easiest way to do that is to e-mail a release to one contact and then "CC" the others, but that is rather impersonal and won't help to nurture a relationship. Instead, personalize each e-mail, but include a note saying, "I have also shared this release with ___ in your bureau/newsroom/ office." That way there won't be any conflicts with more than one person working on the same story if someone decides to use it.

If you haven't yet established a relationship with your local or trade journalists but have done your homework on them and know who covers what, you can still approach them with a press release as a way to build a relationship. The best way to do that is to call the specific journalist and simply introduce yourself and say, "I know you probably haven't seen it, but I sent out a press release today and I would love to send you a personal copy with my contact information so that we could discuss it if you're interested." That way the journalist isn't on the spot ("Did you get my press release?") and you are starting off on the right foot. The journalist may or may not want to use your information, but keep trying in a similarly casual way and a relationship will form.

Remember: Journalists want story leads; you just have to approach them on their own terms.

Hastened Communication

Journalists are extraordinarily busy people who operate under constant deadlines. One of the first things that a PR person should know when dealing with journalists is what their deadlines are. At newspapers, it is usually mid-afternoon, but different kinds of newspaper stories have different kinds of deadlines. Lifestyle articles may have to be written more than a week before they are published, whereas current events stories are written and published within hours. Knowing where you fit in is essential to ensuring your news is timely in the eyes of journalists.

Deadlines for radio and TV stories may depend on whether they are for the morning, noon, evening or late night news broadcast — or for the weekend magazine-style feature news show. For magazines, the pace quickens and may become more frantic just before the monthly deadline, but exactly when that would occur varies at different publications.

Respect journalists' deadlines.

Many beginning PR people would love to be able to "do lunch" when first getting to know a journalist, but that is often not possible. For many print journalists, unless there is someone sitting at the desk next to them, the only communications they have are through e-mail and phone. Most of them prefer it that way. E-mail is good because they can fit it into their day when they need to; phone is for contacting someone immediately. This means voicemails are an absolute must.

Many journalists just don't answer their phones. It's not that they don't want to talk; it's just that they don't have the time. When they get a minute, they check e-mail and listen to voicemails. Often, when trying to track down some bit of information, they will have entire conversations with people via voicemails. So when calling a journalist, for whatever reason, leave a voicemail. If you do get a chance to speak directly with a journalist, understand that their time is incredibly valuable and forgive them if they are short with you. It isn't personal.

Things Journalists Love

We have already mentioned that journalists are primarily concerned with topics they know their readers will find interesting or relevant. Because of that, we know that they are partial to facts, figures, and data that can easily be turned into reader content. Here are a few common types of information that journalists really like to see:

1. **Statistics.** Statistics include facts and figures, and often provide an interpretation or analysis of data. Statistics are an easy way to show the consequence or weight of something, and journalists often cite them to convey the importance of information.

2. **Lists.** Just like this list, lists easily break down important information into small, manageable bits of information. Ranked lists are even better. See the next point.

3. **Top 10 or Bottom 10 Lists.** Either way, ranked lists are an extraordinarily easy thing to turn into content. Whenever an item is ranked, whether it is the best, worst, or runner-up, people are interested — and therefore journalists are interested as well. The challenge for PR people is to make ranked lists relevant to their industry without simply being bids for attention. A home and garden website could put out a top ten list of spring cleaning tips, a law firm could put out a list of things every employer should know before hosting a company party, or a health food store could put out a list of the healthiest foods that no one is eating. The key to these lists is for them to be topical and authoritative.

4. **Quotes.** Quotes can be a very powerful asset, yet most press releases squander the opportunity that quotes afford. In most press releases, quotes are just thinly veiled marketing-speak with the added benefit of positioning a CEO's name in a release. But it is much more powerful when a CEO or other expert actually has something concise and significant to say. If a quote offers quality insight, rather than a sales pitch, and if a journalist thinks he or she couldn't say it better or with more authority, then chances are great that the journalist will use the quote in their article.

5. **Analysis.** Just like statistics, analysis of a topic is great fodder for content. If you have a business in a certain field, it almost goes without saying that you have expertise on topics related to that field. Analysis offers a unique insight into a topic, often in a way that can only come from years of experience, and journalists will be more likely to use information backed by credibility. It also helps identify you as an industry expert that journalists can call on when writing future stories on your industry.

Why Press Releases Aren't Just for the Media

Until now, we've only focused on distributing press releases to the media. While the importance of sharing information with the media should never be discounted, it shouldn't be thought of as the only outlet for your news.

Like the marketer of a women's fashion accessory who at first tried to interest business and advertising/marketing media in his product, your press release may fail if you aren't disciplined in identifying exactly who should receive your release. That's why a little research is necessary not only to identify the right media representatives who should receive your release, but also those outside the media who should be receiving your releases.

While contacting the media is the first step to ensuring that your press release has wide distribution, it also sometimes helps to distribute your news directly to companies or organizations that you feel would be specifically interested in your information. Since the press release format is so particular to journalists, and many non-journalists are not familiar with it, you may want to send a short note introducing your news item and linking to the text of the release rather than simply sending the release.

It sometimes helps to distribute your news directly to organizations.

Consider these examples of other recipients for different types of press releases. In each case, it's important to make sure that they receive the release, rather than simply hoping they view the information as a result of media coverage:

- Information about products for students could be sent directly to schools and parent-teacher associations.

- A press release about a new novel by a local writer is sure to find favor with both libraries, book clubs, and owners of independent bookstores.

- Used car dealers and auto body shops are likely to pay attention to a press release sharing information about products that help with the refurbishing of automobiles.

- A press release about job search guides can be of interest to career centers, especially those on college campuses that assist recent graduates in finding employment.

- Information about Christian educational materials is something that churches and parochial schools will want to know about.

- A press release promoting vacation rentals should spark the interest of a number of vendors planning trips for singles, families, students, church groups, and others.

Know How to Impress Your Audiences

Outside of journalists, there is the audience specific to your industry. Learning how to appeal to that audience is a topic that is beyond the scope of a press release "how-to" e-book. But don't forget that journalists are aficionados, too; otherwise they wouldn't be covering the topics that they do. If you make them excited, then they will pass that excitement on to their readers. And since journalists are well-informed participants in the industries they cover, press releases should speak to them as peers.

Since various professions use specialized language and jargon (medical terminology among physicians, "legalese" among attorneys, etc.), it's important to use this kind of language when writing press releases targeted to professionals in the relevant field. But don't forget that complicated language can be difficult for those who are uninitiated, so sometimes specialized language can be a hindrance. This dilemma can leave even PR professionals stumped, so here are a few guidelines:

The jargon dilemma can leave even PR professionals stumped.

- **Appeal to your base.** If your industry exists within a highly specialized niche, then go with your strong suit. The people who matter will understand.

- **Include a reliable media contact.** Marketing people may not be able to answer highly technical questions, and technical people may not have the knack for putting a PR spin on matters. For press releases that require both technical expertise and diplomacy, a single media contact who is fluent in both areas would best serve the media's needs. For some companies, this is not an option, however; in the absence of a single good representative, identify two media contacts with clearly defined purposes: general and technical. Keep in mind, however, that including more than one media contact can have negative ramifications. Journalists, in general, do not want to hunt down multiple contacts, so to avoid any confusion make sure that any additional contacts have clear roles.

- **Put out two press releases.** If you have a broad audience as well as a niche one, it may be appropriate to put out two press releases, each tailored to a specific audience. A good example would be a set of releases for a new enzyme replacement therapy: one, indulgent with biological processes clinical results, and specialized medical data, while the other discusses general areas like application to fighting certain diseases, and how it will result in new medicines and treatments. When taking this route, issue the technical press release first. Core audiences should always be the first to know.

Most press releases will not have to deal with this problem as most markets don't have language that is so specialized that it is difficult for laypeople to understand, but for those where this is a consideration, speaking the language of your peers is ideal.

Have You Read the Newspaper Lately?

Targeting your press release to the right audience also involves taking the time to stay on top of current events and industry trends by reading newspapers and watching television news, both local and national. It's important to know what's going on, who it affects, and how your expertise and products can benefit the world of today and tomorrow. But remember, your press release still has to be relevant, even when you target it to a particular group because of something that is happening within your community.

Keeping up with the latest news allows you to:

- Be ready when issues, events or trends arise that are relevant to your organization.
- Be on guard if a particular demographic or customer contacts you about breaking news.
- Keep up with what other public relations practitioners are doing.
- Track the reporters who cover the topics and trends you care about.

When you stay on top of current events like mentioned above, you can ensure that you are using your press releases and public relations campaigns to their greatest and most immediate extent.

Section 2:
The Press Release Dissected

Chapter 6

Everything You Need to Know About Writing a Headline

Just the Facts, Ma'am

In the 1960s, the popular TV show *Dragnet* helped coin the enduring phrase, "Just the facts, Ma'am." Even though it's been decades since the show was on air, the phrase is still popular because it's straight to the point, useful, and actually good advice. Certainly when it comes to writing press release headlines, it should be something you take to heart.

Simply put, headlines — regardless of whether they are for a news feature or product release — should focus only on the facts as they relate to the information in the release. That doesn't mean that the headline used for a press release has to be dull, though; they can even be very creative.

Headlines are the first thing that anyone will see of a press release. On the wire, press releases are arranged by category, then there is a list of headlines in chronological order according to when the releases hit the wire. Journalists make a split-second decision whether or not to click on each headline and read the whole press release, or to skip it and move on to something else.

The headline is the most valuable real estate in a press release.

Knowing that, it doesn't take a PR wizard to realize that the headline is the most valuable real estate in an entire press release. So making an effective headline can often be the difference between a press release getting read or not. Luckily, there are three golden rules for effective headlines that will keep your headlines on track for what journalists are looking for:

- Make them informative.
- Make them short.
- Make them relevant.

Don't forget this checklist for making sure the headline of a press release contains "Just the Facts":

- ✓ All pertinent information is included.
- ✓ Information is written in a fashion that's to the point.
- ✓ The information is truthful.

- ✓ There is no fluff.
- ✓ There is no sensationalism.

Informative Headlines

The first and primary task of a headline is to inform journalists what your press release is announcing. This is an absolute basic, but it is often overlooked by press release novices. Think about it as a one-sentence summation of your press release. You can't include every detail in one sentence, but you can include the important stuff, and that's what a headline must embody.

Avoid, however, over-summarizing the information. Readers still have to be able to gain a good understanding of what kind of information they can expect to see when they click on the headline. At the same time, headlines can't give everything away. There has to be an enticement to keep reading.

Let's take a look at an example that is informative, but not informative enough.

Two Hired

The headline might be accurate, but it takes succinctness to an extreme. There's nothing to interest journalists and draw them in to the rest of the information. To improve on this underachievement, let's look at possible versions of the headline with additional words added each time that expand the release's story:

Two Executives Hired

Two Accounting Executives Hired

ABC Co. Hires Two Accounting Executives

ABC Co. Hires Two Former XYZ Co. Accounting Executives

The headline now offers just enough of the 5Ws to warrant proceeding with the rest of the release, where, as surmised from the headline, it is likely a reader will learn who the executives are, what kind of benefits they are expected to bring to the company, how these hires affect ABC Co.'s standing in the industry, etc.

Let's take another look at the evolution of what makes for an effective press release headline by discussing information a policy group might want to share about a new study. Consider this headline:

Group Issues Study

As with the headline of the release announcing the hires, the headline above is accurate, but there's still a lot missing. As it is, there are far too many questions left unanswered: Which group is it? What kind of study is being issued?

To make this headline more informative, there are a number of details that could enhance the message:

Group Issues New Study

Anderson Center Issues New Study

Anderson Center Issues New Study on Home Schooling

Anderson Center Issues New Study on the Impact Home Schooling Has on Student Learning

The last expanded headline answers several questions that are absent from the original, including who conducted the study and what it concerns. The headline strategically leaves out any information about the findings or conclusions of the study and leaves that to be discussed in the body of the release.

Also missing from the headline are any claims that the study is "definitive" or "one-of-a-kind," which may be claims that are not possible to back up. Such claims can be instant turn-offs for journalists. (More on that below.)

Knowing the Industry

Earlier we mentioned that being involved in your industry was a good way to meet journalists and maintain relationships with them. While that is true, it is obviously a secondary benefit to staying involved in your industry. The first benefit is knowing what people in your industry want and what compels them.

Know what people in your industry want and what compels them.

Knowing what customers want is an easy way to identify the newsworthy aspect of a press release so that it can be highlighted in the headline. For instance, the company United Refrigerator is one of many refrigerator manufacturing companies on the market and it wants to put out a press release about a new line of refrigerators. In the release it is likely that all of the benefits and features of the new line will be discussed. Let's say it is the most space-efficient refrigerator on the market, one of the cheapest, has a TV built into the door, and is designed by Artu, the famous Parisian designer.

There are a number of selling points about this line of refrigerators, and that means that there are a number of elements that could be singled out and highlighted for a headline. The obvious choice, however, would be to go general, with something like:

United Refrigerator Unveils New Line of Cheap, Efficient Refrigerators, Designed for Looks and Functionality

While that headline works, it could be more effective. It highlights all of the benefits of the product, but it gets a little muddled in detail and doesn't have an eye-catching interest or hook needed to draw interest from journalists.

One of the ways to remedy this is to find the benefit that consumers are most focused on at the moment and play to that one. That way you can grab the most interest with the headline, then discuss the other benefits later in the release. For example, if efficient use of space is what consumers are focusing on, then an appropriate headline might read:

Spaciousness Defines New Line of United Refrigerator Models

Or if designer refrigerators are all the rage in interior design:

New Artu-Designed United Refrigerator Models Exemplify Contemporary Style

That way you are appealing to the desires of customers (and, for the most part, journalists want to be in the loop on what customers want) and you are maximizing potential interest in the release.

Other Key Headline Points

The most successful headlines are informative and address the *who* and *what* of a press release. The examples above follow this model, starting off with *who* (ABC Co., The Anderson Center, United Refrigerator) and follow up with what they were doing (hiring executives, releasing a study, releasing a new product). This is an easy way to catch the eye of readers with recognizable information or to assert a brand.

For press releases that are announcing new product launches, it's generally a good idea to include the name of the product in the headline. For press releases that aren't announcing a product launch, having at least the name of the company in the headline is a good idea — and some newswires will require it to lend legitimacy to a release.

Making It Short

A headline is the most valuable real estate in a press release, yet it is also the most limited. Although there aren't any formal rules, over the wire or otherwise, stating that a headline has to be within certain parameters, there is a general limitation on how much people will read before they lose interest and move on to something else. This can be a very damning limitation.

There are guidelines, formed in the court of popular opinion, for the appropriate length of a headline:

- Keep headlines to a single, precise statement.
- Use a subhead if you have to. Subheads can help keep essential information up front.

While these are very general guidelines, they are what the members of the media have come to expect.

Length of Headlines

We have already discussed that headlines should be roughly 60-80 characters, a character being a single unit of information on a computer. A character is any letter, number, or punctuation that can be typed. For example, there are four characters between these two brackets, [a4?], the fourth being a space.

The idea behind this limitation isn't to keep headlines within a strict structure, but rather to keep writers thinking like readers. As a writer, there are a lot of elements that you may want people to see and know, but as a reader, you usually just skim headlines to find something that interests you. Even if a long headline contains information that is very interesting, it probably takes too long to convey that information.

Note that some websites that stream press releases from newswires may simply cut off the end of a long headline or subhead. This also happens when search engines refer to your release in response to a search by one of their users. The only control a press release writer has over such truncation is to write concise headlines and subheads.

In the headline, get your information across in as little space as possible.

So the bottom line for headline length is this: Take as much space as you need to get your information across. Just make sure you can get your information across in as little space as possible.

Cutting Down on Space

Headlines aren't exactly sentences. They may use internal punctuation, but do not normally end with a period, question mark or exclamation mark. And even though headlines should still contain the basic elements of a sentence (i.e., a subject and verb), they don't need to contain all of them (e.g., prepositions). This keeps headlines down to a manageable length and reserves limited headline space for important words only.

The following is an example of a headline that is written as if it were a complete sentence:

S Sprockets and C Cogs Announce Arrival of Botlizabeth, the First Official Robotic Impostor to the Throne

While this is a fine headline length (note that it is over the character limit mentioned above), the following is a bit more streamlined for the length-conscious:

S Sprockets, C Cogs Announce Botlizabeth: First Official Robotic Royalty Impostor

The idea is to cut unnecessary words and replace others with shorter synonyms while retaining the same meaning and readability.

Subheads

The subhead of a press release is something of a catch-all. It is for information that is important enough to be singled out, but not important enough to make the cut for the headline. Also, if the headline communicates all of the important information but could use some further explanation, a subhead can fill that role.

Let's take a look at a situation where a subhead would likely come into play:

Computer Corporation Announces New Degaussing Capabilities

The example above is just a headline and would seem to work in that it is concise and informative. But while it is informative, it doesn't provide enough information to attract the attention of journalists. Thus a more informative and attention-grabbing headline might read:

Computer Corporation Announces New Capabilities to Degauss Various Gadgets, Including Cellphones, PDAs, Laptops, PCs, Macs, Satellites, Robots, Tricorders, and Roombas

The expanded headline definitely includes more attention-grabbing information, but the result of adding that information is that the headline is now cluttered. Situations like this are where a subhead can help. Using both a headline and a subhead for this press release would help balance out the information and might read:

Computer Corporation Announces New Degaussing Capabilities for

Various Gadgets

Expanded capability includes cellphones, PDAs, laptops, PCs, Macs, satellites, robots, tricorders, and Roombas.

Making It Relevant

Fluff, sensational wording, or claims that are false or inaccurate can quickly lead to a press release that is dead on arrival. At best, fluff and sensationalism in a headline can lead recipients to downplay its importance once they determine there is little substance to the press release. At worst, they might totally ignore the press release because the headline is too sugar-coated or makes claims that sound implausible.

Be sure to avoid words such as "great," "unbelievable," "mind-boggling," or "incredible." Many PR novices make this mistake, and it is one of the worst that can be made.

It makes perfect sense why novices would want to attempt sensational, cute, and even playful headlines. They know that headlines are gold and you have to do everything you can to entice viewers to click on them so that they will read a press release in its entirety. But in thinking that, novices forget their audiences: journalists. Journalists are told hundreds of times a day that something is the best, will change lives, is amazing, is an unbeatable deal and so on. It is not hard to see why a journalist would ignore yet another sensational headline.

Avoid sensational, cute or even playful headlines.

Don't forget that journalists deal with facts, not games. Sensational headlines are an immediate turn-off for them.

Headlines Containing Fluff/Sensationalism

So what do these fluffy, sensational headlines look like? A press release headline that contains fluff might read like:

Limited Time Only! Amazing Deal on NASA Engineered Golf Clubs from Dan Doh Golf Emporium! Only $399!

There are so many things wrong with this headline it's hard to say where to begin. First, there are the multiple exclamation points, which, again, have no place in a press release. Second, the headline is virtually nothing more than a sales pitch designed to sell more golf clubs. Third, there is the use of the word "amazing," which has the ring of an unsubstantiated claim. Then there is the fact that the headline leads with price.

Another one of those unwritten rules of headlines is that you don't lead with a price. Sure, the point is that you want customers to know that there is a sale going on. And it may be a great sale for great clubs, but you don't just come out and flatly say, "There's a sale, come in and buy stuff." That is marketing. Press releases are public relations. If you are having a sale and you want people to participate, it is best to wrap that information in something more palatable for the press. This is called an angle.

An angle is a way of approaching information. In the example above, the angle is that there is a sale and you want people to buy clubs. That's going nowhere. Journalists have no interest in helping you sell clubs — at least not so blatantly. Still, there is a sale, and you want people to buy those clubs, so it's best to deliver that same information with a different angle, something that the press might find interesting.

An angle is a way of approaching information.

A possible route for this information is already hinted at: NASA-engineered clubs. That's pretty impressive. Why not write a press release about how the science of engineering clubs is dominating the sport, or about how the best players aren't just extremely talented, they have the best science backing them up? Throw in some facts, figures, and other bits of information that journalists love. Then, at the bottom of the release, mention that your store happens to carry some of the more scientifically advanced clubs on the market, and what do you know? They happen to be on sale. Lucky.

A new headline for a story like that might read:

From Persimmon Wood to Polycarbonate Fibers: Dan Doh Golf Emporium's Look at the Science of Modern Golf

Those two headlines couldn't be more different from one another, but they serve the same purpose. And even though the second headline is not as straightforward at the first, the second will almost assuredly sell more golf clubs.

While the first example is far more common than it should be, it is an obvious example of an over-the-top headline. With the next one, let's look at a headline that is still too sensational, but in a more subdued way.

Incredible Technology Provides Best Hope for Millions

The technology is incredible? By whose definition of "incredible"? And will the technology really offer the "best" hope? More important, what is the new technology? And who will be the beneficiary of all this hope?

Sure, it's not as bad as the previous example, but it's still vague about what the technology is and which millions it may help. Simple changes that enhance clarity usually help clear up fluff as well. A revised headline might read:

New Technology from Johns Hopkins Provides Hope to Millions of Cancer Patients

This example gets rid of the unnecessary information and replaces it with concrete facts. Now the impact of the information is substantially clearer.

False/Inaccurate Information

Information in the headline of a press release that is false, outdated or misleading — regardless of whether unintentional or intentional — can not only cause damage to an organization's credibility; it may also create confusion if recipients don't know the truth. Believe it or not, false information can be libelous even if the press release is not used. Possession of the press release might be enough for a defendant to prevail in a legal dispute. That is yet another reason to stick to the facts and keep headlines relevant.

Wrapping Things Up

We'll close our examination of keeping things relevant with some examples of headlines that are false or misleading.

False Headline: New Drug Cures Migraine Headaches

This is fine if the drug actually cures migraines. But the headline contains information that is false if the drug only offers temporary relief from migraine headaches.

Misleading Headline: Proto Dome Electronics Store to Distribute Free DVDs

The headline is misleading if it's subsequently disclosed in the release that the purchase of a DVD player is required to obtain a free DVD. The deception is much like an advertisement that features small print explaining the actual details of a sales item.

Misleading Headline: Conquest Brewery Unveils New Seasonal Brews

As with the other examples, the information in the headline might be correct. But if the brewery is announcing the availability of seasonal brews that can be purchased annually — rather than beers available for the first time — the information is misleading.

Final Thoughts

Along with the basics, there are a few other odds and ends to consider that can either help improve a headline or diminish its impact:

- Journalists often wait until they have written all of a story before deciding on the opening paragraph that summarizes the information. Writing the headline of a press release may demand a similar challenge, so try writing the press release first before going back and reading it and selecting a headline that is appropriate.

- Make the headline of a press release impossible to ignore. The media may not like an individual or organization issuing a release, but a winning headline will make a specific release hard to ignore. Conveying the importance of a press release in a headline helps assure that the release cannot be discarded.

- Don't include hype in the headline that, for example, makes it sound like the press release is promoting a legendary recording artist known worldwide, when the reality is that it's a local singer attempting to make a local name for himself.

- Avoid using jargon or acronyms that may confuse recipients or limit their understanding of information in a press release. Note that this is different in the body of a release where, as was previously mentioned, using language that is commonly shared among members of the target demographic is acceptable.

- Along with questioning whether information in a headline is correct, remember also to check for spelling and grammar. Double-check for consistency — especially in how names are represented. The misspelling of an important person's name in a news story because of an inconsistency in a press release is a difficult error to recall or fix.

Chapter 7

Datelines and Introductory Paragraphs

Demonstrating That You Have Something to Say

"Blessed is the man who, having nothing to say, abstains from giving wordy evidence of the fact." — George Eliot, English novelist (1819 - 1880)

After the headline, the opening paragraph is the second most important part of a press release. Each opening paragraph contains two elements:

- Dateline
- Summarizing Paragraph

Of these two elements, the summarizing paragraph is by far the more important, but the dateline is necessary for all newswires.

Eliot's quote is relevant to the summarizing paragraph because a press release can easily pass the challenge of including an effective headline, only to demonstrate with its first few words that it has nothing to say of any substance. That's why the opening paragraph of a press release must express the 5 Ws in a way that convinces recipients that subsequent paragraphs contain even more relevant information.

Datelines

A dateline is the first line of text after a headline and it is placed at the beginning of the first paragraph. It's also a bit of a misnomer in that is has more information than just the date. Each dateline contains two or three components:

- City
- State (included unless the city is on the AP list of cities that need no state to be mentioned)
- Date

The purpose of the dateline is to give reporters two very key bits of information: where a release is coming from and when it was made available. It's just that simple.

City/State

The point of the city and state information in domestic datelines is to show where the information is coming from: no more, no less. There is a common misconception out there that including a city and state means that a press release is only locally related. That is not the case. Every company, no matter how big, puts the city and state of its headquarters on its press releases — even if the company is in a relatively small city, like Redmond, Washington. But there can be a bit more to it if you want there to be.

Though a dateline has to be there, there are no rules saying that the city and state listed have to be accurate. If your business is in Miami, but you want your release to say it's from Seattle, you can do that. The only question is, why would you? It's usually advisable to keep your dateline close to home, but there are cases when a far-flung dateline is acceptable, such as when your company is attending a trade show in a major metropolitan area and wants to play off the buzz a trade show almost invariably generates.

The only real limitation to a dateline is that the city has to be a place that is real. Press releases can't come from places like Candy Land or Orange County, the latter being a common name for an area, but not an actual city. To be listed as a city in the dateline, a U.S. location must be a town or city with a zip code.

The only reason to bring up being able to list other cities as a city of origin is because it can be reasonable in some cases. Many suburbs of major cities are completely unknown outside of their metro areas, so it is fine for businesses to use the closest major city in their dateline. Most people have probably never heard of Sandy Springs or White Marsh before, but they know about their Metro areas of Atlanta and Baltimore, respectively.

Additionally, there are some cities that are renowned for certain things. If a business participates in that industry but is not located in its major city, it can use that major city as its city of origin. Fashion companies have used New York and Paris as their city of origin, even if they are nowhere near them. As noted, companies participating in a major trade show may wish to use the city where the show is occurring to signal breaking news to the media. Moreover, companies putting out releases about Christmas gifts have used North Pole, Alaska for an extra sense of festivity. (It's an actual town.)

Writing It Out

Just a quick note of reminder on how to write out the city and state in domestic datelines: The city is always written out in full capitals. The state should be written out in the abbreviated AP style, detailed in the AP stylebook (The Associated Press Stylebook and Briefing on Media Law). The wire will change anything that isn't in AP style to the appropriate format before a release is issued.

According to AP style there are a handful of cities, both domestic and international, that do not require having the state or country written out next to them. There are too many to list here, but it is just a small sampling of the world's most populated commercial centers that are easily identifiable — such as LOS ANGELES or LONDON.

Date

The date in the dateline should reflect the date that the press release is distributed, and it is formatted as month, date, year.

Ideally, the month is formatted according to AP style, which abbreviates all the months except for March, April, May, June and July. The wire will insert the properly formatted date automatically if it is omitted or formatted improperly.

If a press release is being manually distributed, to some local journalists for example, then proper attention should be paid to the date. At the beginning of every new year, it is an innocent mistake to type in the previous year instead of the current one. This can be a damaging mistake — why would a journalist pay attention to a release from the past?

After each dateline, include a dash (—) and then begin the first paragraph.

The Summarizing Paragraph

The hardest thing for a headline to do is grab the attention of readers who are skimming a number of headlines and convince them to click on the headline. The summarizing paragraph has a similar job. It has to convince someone who was sold on the headline that the information in the press release is worth reading and legitimate. Following the inverted triangle structure, the summarizing paragraph needs to contain the most important information in the press release. The 5 Ws should be addressed right away and spell out the substance of the press release in a succinct way.

The summarizing paragraph must contain the most important information in the press release.

The basic idea is that someone can read the headline and the opening paragraph and he or she will know what the press release is about because, in many cases, that may be all that will be read. The reader may not know the details and nuances that the body details will disclose, but he or she will know enough to state the purpose of a press release definitively.

This is, again, a way in which a press release is not fiction or an article. The people reading press releases don't want to be wrapped up in suspense waiting for the big reveal at the end. In press releases, you tell readers the most important things they need to know in the first few sentences and then flesh out the details in the body.

Here is a sample summarizing paragraph:

Amai Chocolates, San Francisco's oldest family-run chocolatier, announced the launch of its new line of chocolates, SweetCakes(TM). The new SweetCakes(TM) are a variant on the traditional ganache-filled truffle, and are instead filled with moist balls of cake, coated in chocolate, to retain the well-known truffle shape. The new line comes in many assorted combinations of cake and chocolate to appease any palette. A full list of flavor combinations and boxes for purchase is available at http://www.amaichocolate.com.

After an opening paragraph like this, the body might go on to discuss reasons why the new sweets are special, what the inspiration was to make them, more details on their availability, and so forth.

Possible Considerations

By now, we have already discussed the 5 Ws in detail and their proper application should be well understood. They are key in making an opening paragraph stick to the facts and deliver, in concentrated form, the purpose of a press release. There are, however, other pieces of information beyond the 5 Ws that an opening paragraph can include. These are elements that aren't necessary for every press release, but they do come up and can help when the time is right.

Timeliness. Unlike *when*, timeliness is more relative. It is usually used to tie the information in a press release to current events.

In order to celebrate the 60th anniversary of the founding of the U.S. space program, Dobsonian Astronomics announces the "Sailing Under the Stars" boat tour and dance, starting July 29th. The two-day, one-night tour will take guests from Cape Canaveral deep out into the ocean, away from any city lights, for a late night dance under the stars.

Proximity. Even when a press release is distributed nationally, if it will be of greatest interest to locals, it is best to play up that local aspect.

Simple Style, a Denver-based fashion company that has been owned and operated by Denver natives since 1940, has received the state commerce secretary's "Colorado Spirit" award. The award celebrates businesses that truly epitomize the Colorado spirit of ruggedness and free will.

Prominence. Like in the example above, prominence puts a spotlight on some area of prestige or unique importance. Press releases that can focus on prominence usually announce awards, endorsements, or are in some way tied to a person, place, thing, or event of note.

Packing and Trading, Inc. announces the hiring of William Jones, Jr. as executive CEO. Mr. Jones is a long-standing fixture in the import and export business and will bring a lifetime of experience to the company. His family has been involved with shipping since the 1850s, in Victorian England.

Consequence. A press release also may need to explain at the outset the implications of critical information. Like a news story, the opening paragraph should define the significance of certain information to a broad demographic or community.

Due to poor end-of-year returns, the Tierell Corporation is having to scale back production of its synthetic cotton ties six percent. The cutbacks will mean that up to 500 people will either be let go or forced into retirement.

Human Interest. Dealing with human interest means the inclusion of details that spark compassion or empathy. Make sure the opening paragraph of a human interest release contains such details.

Every year a small but increasing number of children are diagnosed with secondary aphasia, keeping them from being able to speak and comprehend language. Due to its relative rarity, these children are often left in the care of those who try their best, but aren't specifically trained to handle the unique needs of aphasia children. That's why Preston Education, along with the Johnson Medical Center, has announced the creation of the Joyce Moore Educational Institute.

While the previous examples each address timeliness, proximity, prominence, consequence, or human interest, it's also possible for the opening paragraph of a press release to include several of those considerations at once.

C83 Films announced that filming has been scheduled for next week [timeliness] in several locations across Virginia [proximity] for the movie adaptation of John Grisham's [prominence] latest novel, which will star Tom Cruise [prominence].

This Is Something That You've Just Got to Hear!

The first few words of a press release can catch the eyes of its recipients with the inclusion of wording that creates excitement. Consider the opening statements below. Both start off dull, but are followed by slightly different — and more effective — versions:

Dull: A new flight simulator at the U.S. Space and Rocket Center simulates the effects of weightlessness.

Better: Visitors to the U.S. Space and Rocket Center can experience the unequalled feeling of weightlessness in a new flight simulator.

Dull: Callahan Tire announced the new PrimaGrip(TM) snow chains. The patented design allows for maximum grip and durability in snowy conditions.

Better: Callahan Tire announced its new premium snow safety product, the PrimaGrip(TM) line of snow chains. The new chains were patented with a first-of-its-kind design made to optimize tire grip and chain durability.

Getting It Right the First Time

We'll conclude our look at how to make sure the first paragraph of a press release conveys its importance with a few more suggestions:

- Never begin a press release with a quote. This is not only awkward, it rarely summarizes the importance of information in a release.

- Like a headline, the opening paragraph should sell recipients of a press release on its information. The first lines offer another chance to reel in readers if the headline has failed. The chances of sparking their curiosity starts to diminish quickly after that.

- Avoid an opening paragraph that is a half-page in length. The paragraph should be packed with details, but a good writer knows how to accomplish that by using a minimum amount of words.

- Review the opening paragraph after the entire release has been written to guarantee that it does not contradict any information that follows.

- Just like with a headline, it may be better to write the full body of a press release first, and then go back to write the opening paragraph. That way you can simply review all of the important points and put them together in a way that conveys the message of the release in only a few sentences.

Chapter 8

Writing the Body of a Press Release

Elements of a Body

Well here it is: the body of a press release. After putting in all that effort to grab people's attention with concise headlines and well-rounded opening paragraphs, there's the open range of the press release body. After dealing with strict suggested guidelines of character limits and that nagging reminder to stay focused and say only what needs to be said, now you can just let it all out and write to your heart's content, right? It's time for the world to know every little thing about what you have deemed newsworthy. Isn't that right?

Not quite.

It's true that compared to writing a headline and opening paragraph, writing the body paragraphs is not nearly as restrictive. However, to think that you can just let loose and write anything is an idea that will get you into a lot of trouble fast.

When it comes to writing the body of a press release, there are a couple points to keep in mind:

Keep it short and focused.

- Keep it short.
- Stay focused.

While that may seem a little difficult, if not somewhat contradictory, it is the primary conflict of all press release writing.

Will You Please Get to the Point Now?

When Irish playwright George Bernard Shaw famously apologized for writing a long letter because he "did not have time to write a short one," he described a dilemma often encountered in press release writing.

While sharing information is easy when including every detail, it is more difficult to summarize the same information in a fashion that is both brief and yet still conveys the entire message of a press release. Shaw was sharing with the recipient of his letter that while it might take him time to write a long letter, he would have to put even more effort into writing a shorter letter that summarized the same information.

What are some of the reasons why long press releases should be avoided? Consider these few:

1. It can be more difficult for readers to understand the message that you are attempting to share.

2. Lengthy press releases increase a writer's chance of losing focus.

3. Wordiness drastically increases the likelihood that journalists won't read an entire press release.

The average press release length is somewhere around three to five paragraphs long. That translates to a word count of 350 to 500 words. Keep in mind, though, that the word count includes everything written in a press release (from the headline to the contact information), not just the body paragraphs. Microsoft Word includes a handy Word Count feature, which can usually be found under Tools.

Omit repetitive information and words that sugarcoat the main ideas of the release.

Keeping a press release brief involves, among other things, knowing how to use words. When it comes to brevity, the key is to refrain from extraneous use of modifiers, along with omitting information that is repetitive and words that sugarcoat the main ideas of the release.

When writing anything, it's crucial to remember the rule of quality over quantity. That's why extra words don't always enhance the meaning of information in a press release and can diminish its impact.

A public relations professor was known for telling his students about one of his friends to illustrate the importance of keeping a press release brief.

"What she said was usually important, it's just that she included so many details that it took her minutes to tell me things that she could have shared in seconds.

"Rather than saying it was crowded at the mall, she had to identify everyone who was there and how long she waited in line — often going off on tangents about what she was thinking while she was waiting."

For press releases, the challenge is not to take pages but just a few sentences to convey information that can be neatly summarized into a select number of paragraphs.

Brevity

Achieving brevity means avoiding certain traps. Let's finish our discussion of keeping press releases short and to the point with a few more suggestions:

- Say the same thing with fewer words. Words such as "really" in front of "excited," for example, are unnecessary. The active voice can also be helpful in keeping a press release brief. Rather than saying "New safety procedures have begun to be initiated by the company," word your release so that it reads, "The company has initiated new safety procedures."

- Eliminate any wording that is not definitive or attributed. An example would be writing "Experts say crime will increase," rather than saying that "Crime may increase, according to several individuals familiar with law enforcement practices."

- Rather than using jargon on first reference and explaining it later, start by sharing information in language that everyone will easily grasp. Jargon, you will recall, is specialized industry terminology.

- Convey the importance of information by summarizing it in a neat package. Redundant phrases such as "outdated equipment that is no longer useful," or "wet, rainy weather," drag a press release down.

- Share your information without using hype. Hype is like empty calories found in sweets. For example, "the most innovative product to come along since sliced bread" does not really inform anyone. Along with turning off editors, hype fattens up your press release with no benefit.

- Make sure that information isn't so buried in the release that its recipients believe there's nothing there. You should strive to bring important information to the front of the press release in hopes your reader will do the same when developing his or her story.

Make the 5 Ws Easy to Find

The key to writing concisely is to stay focused on your topic. Remember that the best way to stay focused on a topic is to stick to the 5 Ws. Each press release should cover only one newsworthy bit of information, and sticking to the 5 Ws is the best way to delve fully into the newsworthy aspects of that one bit of information.

We talked earlier about highlighting prominence, consequence, human interest, etc. in the opening paragraph, but now let's look again at how stressing the 5 Ws can increase the visibility of information as well as make it shorter.

Who

Organizers of Booramoo Music Festival announced a line-up for this year's festival that they believe will appeal to a broad demographic.

"I'm excited about this year's acts," said Booramoo Chairman Kip Gerrold. Scheduled to appear are Donna Summer, Three Dog Night, Willie Nelson, and The Black Keys.

These three sentences can be condensed and the *who* emphasized early by writing:

Organizers of Booramoo Music Festival are excited about this year's eclectic line-up, which includes Donna Summer, Three Dog Night, Willie Nelson, and The Black Keys, because they believe it will appeal to a broad demographic.

What

The Concord bicycle was made to fill an obvious void that the current market wasn't addressing.

Everyman Bicycles saw how bicycle companies were specializing their market. Every bike had to be optimized for road or racing. Bicycles were being improved for bicycling enthusiasts, but regular people who just want a way to get around were being left out in the cold. With every new improvement came new costs, keeping all but the bottom-shelf brands out of the reach of most customers.

Everyman Bicycle's new Concord bike offers function, durability, and affordability, aimed at the regular consumer, who cares about price and reliability more than space-age polymers.

While none of this is particularly bad information, it takes too long to get to the information that matters, and then doesn't even state that information in the most effective way. Here is a crisper version.

Everyman Bicycle's new Concord line of bicycles is designed with the average consumer in mind, offering durability and function at a price that is accessible for everyone. Unlike the kinds of bikes that now rule the market, which are so focused on performance that the average bicycle is well beyond the wallets of most, the Concord is stripped down to the essential functions.

When

Due to severe cutbacks, Gum-tion's most popular flavor of chewing gum, Hyper Mint, is planned to be discontinued. Even though the flavor is the most popular that Gum-tion has ever produced, it is by far the most expensive to make, more than four times as much as all other flavors combined.

"We understand that Hyper Mint is deeply loved by our customers, that's why we encourage them to stock up while it is still in production," said Gum-tion president, Chicle Ruse. "It's unfortunate that Hyper Mint will soon be out of production forever, but we just can't handle the costs anymore. So for all you Hyper Mint lovers out there, get as much of it as possible while you still can."

Gum-tion first introduced Hyper Mint back in the 1960s.

Though a rather extreme example, it is astounding how frequently the most important information in a release can be so easily overlooked. Those who love Hyper Mint so much that they would go out and stockpile it would undoubtedly want to know when it was going to go out of production and wouldn't be satisfied with "soon." Here is one way to fix this weakness:

Due to severe cutbacks and prohibitive costs, Gum-tion's most popular flavor of chewing gum, Hyper Mint, is scheduled to be discontinued this January when the current contract with suppliers expires and on-hand ingredients are exhausted.

Hyper Mint is by far the most expensive product to produce that Gum-tion makes, costing four times as much as all other flavors combined.

Where

Jackson Pharmaceuticals will provide free flu shots to senior citizens throughout Hinds County, Mississippi from November 1 through December 10.

Jackson Pharmaceuticals is offering the shots to guard against this year's flu strain that may be harmful to elderly residents. Shots will be available at all county libraries and hospitals.

By addressing *where* earlier in the release, the following rewrite not only gets to the facts of the matter more quickly, it eliminates the need for a second paragraph.

Jackson Pharmaceuticals is offering free flu shots at all Hinds County libraries and hospitals from November 1 through December 10 to help senior citizens guard against this year's flu strain.

Why

Marilyn's Grocery chain will be closed all day Christmas Eve and Christmas Day, with customers urged to pick up all holiday foods before closing on Tuesday, Dec. 23.

"We value our customers and hope that they will remember to take home the many holiday favorites that can add to their holiday meals," said Marilyn's CEO Jack Norment.

Norment said the grocery stores are closing early to allow employees to spend more time with their families during the holidays.

Why would a grocery store be closed all day when it will inconvenience customers? By explaining that the decision was made to benefit employees, the press release may help encourage customers, in the spirit of Christmas, to work around the inconvenience of having to pick up their food early.

Marilyn's grocery chain will be closed all day Christmas Eve and Christmas Day, allowing employees to spend the holiday with their families. Customers are urged to pick up all holiday foods before closing on Tuesday, Dec. 23.

Remember, even after journalists know what a press release is about after reading a headline and opening paragraph, they don't have a lot of time to search for the pertinent information in a press release. Stick to the main topics and address them right away, explaining their details later in the paragraph. That way it's like each paragraph has its own headline, grabbing readers' attention and telling them the important information, which is followed up by details in subsequent sentences.

Body Building

Outside of body length restrictions, there are a few other things to consider that are relevant only for body paragraphs.

What They Said

Quotes are a staple of press releases, but they are seldom used in the way that most journalists want them to be. Most people who are writing press releases just throw a quote in the second paragraph because it seems like it needs it, and the same is true for larger companies — even companies with large PR firms or their own PR department. A company may simply throw a quote into a press release as a way to get a CEO's name in the release and make that executive sound smart.

The truth is that despite how often people use quotes in press releases, they aren't always necessary. Quotes should be used to add something unique to a press release, like insightful analysis or a concise quip from an executive or an expert. If that isn't what a quote is bringing to a press release, then what is the point of having it in there?

That said, having a good quote from someone prominent that actually adds something to the press release is great. As mentioned earlier, journalists love quotes, and if there is an outstanding quote, journalists will take it straight from the release and use it in their articles.

Journalists love quotes.

An example of a quote that adds to a release would be:

"Relying on composite images to help diagnose patients with injuries that can't be seen has always been a limitation, and current technology always just looks at how to make the previous technology better, not at what a doctor needs. That's why when we started designing the 2501 System, we started from scratch and focused on what a doctor needs to diagnose a patient confidently. The result is a whole new kind of imaging system that eliminates the diagnostic gap between a patient and an image," said CEO Susan Shays.

However, skip the quote if it only reads, "Our new imaging software can be instrumental in helping physicians and other health care officials." The first example conveys a robust understanding of why this new system is unique and the reasoning behind its creation, while the second doesn't add significant information or perspective.

If quoting someone who is not a company employee, make sure to identify the person relative to his or her title, expertise, or life experience as a way of explaining why he or she is being quoted.

While most press release quotes from company executives were written by PR practitioners and not the executives, it is important that every executive approves and understands any quote you have developed for him or her. It is not enough that the company approve the press release if the executive later denies having uttered the quote.

U.S. Senator Thad Bowerton, who served two tours of duty in Vietnam, and is head of the Committee on Armed Services, expressed great interest in the product, saying, "Safety is our biggest priority in any conflict, and we are always looking for new ways to make our troops as safe as possible. This Mithril armor is exactly the kind of thing we look for to protect our service men and women: light enough to keep movement free, but strong enough to withstand heavy attack and save lives."

Avoid Redundancy

Information in a press release can be wordier than necessary when it repeats itself unnecessarily. And if you don't believe that, do a quick re-read of the previous sentence!

Consider this example of how redundancy diminishes the impact of a press release and makes it longer than it has to be:

With the new office and storage facility, the way that Discount DVD operates will change entirely. Nothing will operate the same way.

Now that the move from the old facility is finished, Discount DVD is back in full service, but it was a challenge since the new facility changed the way that employees work entirely.

"It was a little difficult at first. We had been at our old location for so long that we could complete orders with our eyes closed if we wanted to. Now, with the new layout and bigger floor space, we are having to relearn everything. It's like the way that we operate has changed entirely," said CEO Robert Corner.

Another mistake to avoid in press releases is repeating information in the boilerplate elsewhere in the release or identifying someone more than once. For press releases, repeating information is not so much a sin of style as it is a distraction that keeps readers from seeing other information sooner.

Chapter 9

Calls to Action, Boilerplates, and Contact Information

The Last Few Steps

After writing the bulk of a press release, there are still a few matters to take into consideration to help complete the document. Most are optional or specific to the information in a release, but others are required across the board.

When finishing a press release, keep the following elements in mind:

- A call to action
- Important event information
- Boilerplate
- Contact information
- Triple pound or end mark

Call to Action

The call to action can move people in the right direction.

What do you want your press release to do next? What's the point? What's the agenda? Do you want people to visit your website, buy a product, start planning for an event, or subscribe to a service? The reasons why a business would put out a press release are infinite, but one factor is true in the case of all press releases: No one wants someone to read one and then forget about it or move on. Press releases are written so that something will happen, and a call to action can move people in the right direction.

Just as with all other aspects of press releases, a call to action shouldn't be hinted at, suggested, or spirited in under the radar. A call to action should be stated plainly in a way that is easy to find. After all, there was a lot of work that went in to an attractive headline, a captivating opening paragraph, and an enlightening body, all of which are very informative if done right. By the time someone reading a press release reaches the end, the reader should have taken in a lot more information than he or she realizes, so don't just let that person sit on it. Give him or her a convenient outlet for all of the information that has been absorbed.

A call to action is usually short, around a sentence, and is separate from the body paragraphs. A common one would look something like:

For more information, visit the company's website at

http://www.website.com.

The example is simple and straight to the point. It should not get much more complicated than that. See these following examples for some other common calls to action.

Please send all donations to The Wier Fund, PO Box 742, Springfield, VT 05156, or see the secure donation form at http://www.wierfund.org.

The Saxamaphone can be found at all music stores and major online markets. It can also be bought directly from http://www.saxamagic.com.

Event Information

At this point, the 5 Ws have been mentioned enough that they should feel like old friends. With event information, though, referencing the 5 Ws isn't quite the same as any other time 5 Ws need to be employed, and there are usually just three of them rather than five. Just like with the call to action, listing event information is a way to mobilize a reader.

Event information is, like the call to action, presented simply. It is a what/when/where list of the most important information, delineated plainly for easy viewing. This is an option in press releases for events like concerts, webinars and conference calls, corporate functions, etc.

WHAT: "The Importance of Pure Thought" Water Purification Seminar

WHEN: Tuesday, April 7th, 1 p.m. to 5 p.m.

WHERE: Broadway Heights Hotel, Ball Room, 5135 Kensington Ave, St. Louis, MO

Listing information in such a way is not necessary for most releases. In fact, it is not something that is seen all that often, especially coming from small businesses. Keep in mind that journalists are skimming, and your headline and opening paragraph may be the only place to get your core message in front of them. This means that in most cases, you should try to fit as much of the essential event information as possible in the headline and opening paragraph.

Listing event information separately can be coupled with a call to action, though it isn't always necessary. When space is a consideration, choose the one that is the most informative.

For instance, the following event-related information is concise and appropriate for a release that focuses on an author's whole book tour:

For a full schedule of Kilgore Trout's book signing tour for "The Era of

Hopeful Monsters," visit http://www.troutorsturgeon.com/tour.

However, you might use this version when the release highlights the first appearance on the author's book tour:

WHAT: Kilgore Trout's premiere signing of "The Era of Hopeful Monsters"

WHEN: Friday, November 6, 7 p.m.

WHERE: Buchhandlung-V Book Store, 857 Truro Street, Ilium, New York 12180

Boilerplate

It goes without saying that small business owners or PR professionals know who they are and what their businesses do. But a small business is seldom well-known outside of its immediate circle of influence. That is why it is a good idea to include a boilerplate at the bottom of each press release.

A boilerplate is a short paragraph that explains the identity of a company and helps build name recognition among the media. It is a short introduction for the purposes of background information. Boilerplates are meant to be stock language that appears at the bottom of a release. Certainly, they can be updated with new information about the company when appropriate, but they are supposed to be definitive. Media should be able to cut and paste the boilerplate text without any worries about whether the content is up to date or accurate.

Keep boilerplate short and general.

A good boilerplate should address the key questions that journalists could have about your company if they have never heard of you before. Keep it short and general. Topics can include how long the company has been in business, the services you provide, the products you make, and any other unique or identifying bit of information. Don't load it down with corporate-speak and remember that you must be conscientious about space, so aim for around 50 words; keep it under 100.

Here is a sample from a major corporation.

About Whirlpool

Whirlpool Corporation is the world's leading manufacturer and marketer of major home appliances, with annual sales of over $11 billion, 68,000 employees, and nearly 50 manufacturing and technology research centers around the globe. The company markets Whirlpool, KitchenAid, Brastemp, Bauknecht, Consul and other major brand names to consumers in more than 170 countries. Additional information about the

Boilerplates aren't always necessary. They are a good idea to use to help build recognition, but there are occasions where they can be left off without worry. For one, if length is an issue and you have to decide between cutting out information from a release or getting rid of the boilerplate, sacrifice the boilerplate. Don't forget, newswires will take a press release of almost any length, but after a certain cut-off point (which differs depending on the wire or third-party service), extra words mean extra costs and challenges to ultimate readability.

Another reason to omit a boilerplate would be if the information that is usually found in a boilerplate is already in the press release.

Contact Information

Including contact information in a press release is an absolute requirement. Lack of contact information is one of the elements that will keep a release from being distributed over the wire. Obviously, if a press release is submitted without contact information to the wire or a third-party distributor, the distribution service will do what it can to rectify the situation and obtain your contact information. But make no mistakes about it: If there is no contact information, that release is going absolutely nowhere.

A standard set of contact information includes:

- Name
- Title
- Phone Number
- E-mail

This pretty much speaks for itself, but there are a couple of tricks to each item of the contact information, so let's go over them briefly.

Name

This should be the name of the person who is serving as mediacontact. It is the person whom the media will ask for if they need to know something or want to talk about the information in a press release. That means that a media contact shouldn't just be anyone; it should be a person who can represent the company and speak with confidence to the media.

There can be multiple contacts for a press release — but only when necessary. If a company releases a very technical product, it might be a good idea to have a PR contact for general questions and a technical contact for technical questions.

Title

Nothing novel about this one: Just list the press contact's title within a company or organization. Reporters like to know the position of the contact.

Phone Number

A phone number is required by most distribution services.

It's set up this way because journalists, who are always in a hurry, need the fastest way to get in contact with someone if they need to confirm some information.

The numbers that are listed shouldn't be general switchboard numbers but should go directly to the media contact or to a gatekeeper who can easily connect a journalist to the media contact. The number should be one that someone actually answers consistently — even, when possible, after business hours.

As noted earlier, for some people privacy is a concern, and that is a perfectly legitimate concern. If that's the case however, there is an option that has worked well for many. Have a separate number for press releases and let any calls go straight to voicemail. Doing this means that you have to pay close attention to messages after issuing a press release and return any urgent voicemails. Journalists call because they are trying to get in touch with someone quickly, not because they want to wait around for a return call. If you wish to go this route, voicemail service can be purchased online for a very reasonable monthly fee.

E-mail

If a journalist is trying to get in touch with you and it isn't an urgent issue, he or she will most likely try to contact you through e-mail.

If spam is an issue for you, find out whether or not your press release distribution service protects contact information against being harvested by spambots, as eReleases does. This should help, although there is nothing to prevent someone from reading your release and adding your e-mail address to their list without your permission.

If you are worried about spam or privacy, one trick is to set up a dummy account. Web-based e-mail services like Gmail, Yahoo or Hotmail, or an address you create from your own domain, can serve as special e-mails for media contacts. You can have e-mails that have been sent to the dummy addresses forwarded to your primary mail client as long as needed. Afterward, you can disable or simply close down the dummy account. It's easy enough to set up numerous e-mail accounts like "pr2010" to keep your personal e-mail account from being inundated with spam.

Keep in mind, however, that when press releases are archived online, those dummy e-mail addresses could be clicked on by someone who wants to know more even though you thought the time had passed for any interest.

In any event, e-mail needs to be checked frequently after you have distributed a press release.

What Else Can Be Included

For most press releases, the contact information that was just covered is more than adequate for the media. There are, however, a few occasions when extra modes of contact are required. Like with using multiple contacts, this contact information is very rarely needed, and when any of them are needed, they should be used for a well-defined purpose.

Fax

Though they were once the height of technological advancement for press releases, fax machines are antiquated at this point. It is exceedingly rare that the media would still use fax as a form of communication. That said, there are times when a fax is needed, so feel free to list a fax number in those instances. If you can't think of any reason why you would need a fax, then omit the number.

Cell Phone

Companies that have dedicated PR people may include a cell phone number in case he or she cannot be reached through a regular contact number. Having an available cell phone number for the press has worked out for some PR people, but in many of those cases, that cell phone number was given out privately to journalists with whom the PR representative had built up a relationship.

As an alternative to buying another cell phone that is dedicated to business/PR, you can obtain a toll-free number that redirects to an existing cell phone. Services like Kall8 (http://www.kall8.com) can set up a toll-free redirect for a nominal fee a month plus minutes. Like a dummy e-mail account, the service can be shut off or redirected to another number or voicemail (which is included with the service) when it is no longer needed.

After Hours Contact

News breaks at all hours. That's a fact that journalists constantly have to deal with and, by extension, so too do PR people. When a story is just too good and a journalist has to get in contact with someone, no matter the time, that's when the after-hours contact comes in to play. Most major corporations and many publicly traded companies post an after-hours number for their PR professionals.

Exactly who should be an after-hours contact requires careful consideration. The person has to be someone who both doesn't mind receiving phone calls at any hour and can represent the company well, even after being jolted from sleep or dragged from family time.

Use this only if the information in your press release is big or very timely. Beware: An after-hours number allows journalists to be able to upset your routine in an attempt to cover a story.

Finishing Up

You've done everything now. Almost. There is only one more thing to do to put the finishing touches on the press release that you have spent so much time working on and developing into something that has a good shot at attracting attention. All that needs to be done now is to add three little characters:

# # #

This is how you signify that you have reached the end of a press release. Absolutely nothing can go after it. Anything else that comes after the triple pound signs is not a part of the release and won't be transmitted over the wire.

When looking at press releases online, you may notice a few items that follow the triple pound, but that is just distribution information that is automatically added by the wire. It is nothing of concern to press release writers.

The end mark or triple pound (written with spaces in between the pounds and centered, ideally) is simply a unique organization of characters that has a very low chance of occurring naturally in a press release, so it can't be confused as possible content.

Images and Other Extras

Newswires may offer you the option of including images with your release, and they may include that with their service or levy an additional charge for it. The image may be a product photo, a corporate logo, a head shot of a person discussed in the release, or even a diagram or drawing.

Sometimes images are mainly window dressing, but in other cases, an image can do more than attract the attention of media people and prospective customers. In some instances, an image helps clarify a key element in the story and explains it better than words.

An image can help clarify a key element in the story and explain it better than words.

For example, an image of an innovative new product may get across what it looks like far more vividly than your description in words. However, keep in mind that some venues that stream your release will not be showing any images. Therefore, never assume your image is going to convey your story for you.

Be sure to submit a caption along with any photo or image that identifies what it depicts. Your distribution service may also include the opportunity to show a certain page of your web site alongside your release. This could be either your home page or another page that is specifically related to the topic of your release.

A Note About Privacy

One of the concerns that many people have about transmitting contact information over the wire is that it can be seen by parties who aren't journalists and used maliciously or by predatory marketers.

When sending press releases over the wire, those releases aren't just visible on the wire's website. Other news organizations with websites may stream the wire feed and list all of the press releases that are issued over the wire. This means that press releases are essentially public information that can be seen by anyone.

While this can be a problem, it often isn't. Press release contact information is not as a rule the go-to area for scammers and phishers to extract information. However, privacy is always a concern and there are steps that can be taken to ensure it. We have discussed some tactics that can be employed to lessen the impact of spam and annoying phone calls. However, they can't always keep contact information out of the hands of the people who may want to be a nuisance.

There is another option to keep contact information out of the hands of non-journalists, though it isn't always a good idea. When releasing a press release over the wire, there is the option to have the contact information suppressed. This isn't something that is plainly indicated, so it must be requested when dealing with the wire or a third-party distributor.

Suppressing contact information essentially makes it so that only people with access to the wire's website (which generally is strictly limited to registered members of the media) will be able to see the contact information. When other sites stream the releases content publicly, the contact information simply won't be included. It is an unfortunate reality, however, that dedicated shysters can pose as journalists on the wire's website, and not all news websites follow the rules and remove contact information when they are supposed to. The system is not perfect.

Press contact suppression may seem like a good option, but realize that press and business opportunities can come from many places that aren't on the wire. If you limit who can see your contact information, you are essentially cutting off the potential of someone running across your release online, being interested in it, and trying to contact your company for more information. This probably happens with about the same frequency as any malicious actions taken with the same information.

So know that you have the option of protecting your contact information, but also know that it comes at a cost.

When to Send Them

Now that you know everything there is to know about writing and formatting a release, you may be wondering when the best day of the week is to send them. The quick answer is that any weekday can be appropriate. The major newswires operate every day of the week but most journalists (excluding those that cover breaking news) work only Monday through Friday.

Monday is the busiest day of the week for press releases.

Monday is the busiest day of the week when it comes to press releases. Friday is the lightest day, and many publicists prefer to avoid Fridays in the belief that most reporters are thinking about their weekend rather than about new stories to tackle. For that very reason, some companies, as well as the government, like to issue "bad news" press releases on Fridays so as to get less attention for it. As a rule, it doesn't work. Publicly-traded companies that issue poor results after the close of the market on Friday still get clobbered in after hours trading. The bad news turns into Monday headlines.

The second busiest day of the week is Tuesday. This means that if you are looking for a day when you are competing with fewer other releases, yet reporters are still mentally "on the job," you should think about Wednesday or Thursday. However, my personal belief is that there is no magic day to send a press release. If there was, it would become the worst day to send press releases as most people would overwhelm journalists on that day with their press releases.

Whichever day of the week you decide on, press releases usually go out before 9 a.m. Eastern time. If you have a reason for wanting a release to go out at a particular time of day, the wires can schedule your press release for a particular time.

Section 3:
SEO Press Releases

Chapter 10

Publicity Through Web 2.0, Social Media, and SEO Press Releases

Press Releases in the 21st Century

As described up till now, the process of writing and distributing press releases has remained largely unchanged from the process that existed 50 or 60 years ago. Though the specific manner in which press releases have been distributed has been remarkably adaptive to changing technologies, the underlying steps are the same at they have ever been.

As a press release writer, you write a press release intended for journalists and specific industry audiences, and you distribute it over the wire and possibly directly to some close contacts. Then those journalists assess whether your information is beneficial to their audience and turn it into content. Finally, members of your intended audience hopefully read/watch/listen to that content and are influenced by it in a way that is beneficial to you and your business.

In the 21st century, however, the way that we consume content is rapidly changing. Traditional media outlets like television and newspapers are declining and giving way to new media — ones that allow not only a new way to consume content, but a whole new avenue for creating content. This change didn't simply happen because of a preference for new media over old. Rather, it reflects a fundamental change within society regarding how media and content are consumed.

The Internet has created a new media alternative — the SEO press release.

Of course, when discussing this change, we are referring to the rise and prevalence of the Internet in daily life and its influence on content. While the Internet as a medium has transformed press release distribution, it has also spawned a revolution in the pace at which content is consumed. In short, the Internet has created a new media alternative — the SEO press release, which is a uniquely Internet-based method of writing and distributing press releases.

"SEO" stands for "search engine optimization," which is the process of shaping and releasing information online so as to increase search engine traffic. With SEO press releases, you are not only crafting a press release so as to work for you with the search engines, but also using the Internet as your sole means of press release distribution, bypassing newswire services and journalists for the most part. There are pros and cons to this method (to be discussed later), but SEO press releases exist as a way to take advantage of the new methods of content consumption so that you can have direct, unmediated contact with your audience. As with any emerging practice, there is a new set of rules and guidelines that must be learned in order to construct an effective online PR strategy.

To reap the benefits of SEO press releases fully, you must invest a considerable amount of forethought and preparation in the execution of each press release's writing and distribution. An SEO press release may look like a regular press release that is just posted online, but SEO press releases are special in that they are tailor-made to thrive in an online environment. To make something that will thrive in an online environment, you have to understand that environment and why certain pieces of content succeed while others don't.

SEO press releases are created to promote online visibility. A properly crafted SEO press release uses optimized keywords, originality, authority, and elements of importance to its advantage. These collected benefits enhance the visibility of a press release online so that its information can be more easily found by users. But that is not all that an SEO press release is.

SEO press releases rely on the social media communities to help further advance the visibility of their information.

One of the hallmarks of how people are consuming content differently online is that people seek out the information they want and leave everything else alone. When users see something they like, they can use various programs and websites called social media websites to increase the visibility of that information by sharing, spreading, and ranking it within numerous online communities. By increasing the visibility of specific types of content, these communities ensure that such content will thrive and be consumed by more people. More so than traditional releases, SEO press releases rely on these social media communities to help further advance the visibility of their information.

Unlike traditional press releases where once a press release is distributed, it is out of the hands of the distributor, SEO press releases can achieve greater visibility and reach for consumers with the distributor's active and favorable participation in social media communities. Unlike traditional press releases, which depend on journalists and media outlets for visibility, originators of SEO press releases can engineer and encourage visibility.

Social media participation relies on frequent goodwill and community recognition. Thus, to be effective, joining a social media community can't be something you start just hours or days before you post a press release. You must devote time and effort to the process. Likewise, the written SEO press release requires carefully considered and researched wording, along with specialized knowledge of website design and encoding.

In the segments ahead, we discuss the elementary intricacies of a successful SEO press release and the corresponding components of a social media distribution campaign. But keep in mind that it is the nature of the Internet to change constantly. This information is intended to get you started with a rudimentary understanding of SEO press releases, how they work, and how you can make them work for you. Even so, to stay competitive, you must remain current and be flexible enough to learn, drop things that aren't working, and take a few risks. Needless to say, proceed with implementing an SEO campaign only when you feel comfortable with the entire process.

Words of Caution

SEO press releases are continuing to lose their favor with Google. In mid-2013, Google announced that links within press releases should be "no follow" links. Press releases should not influence search engine results. This is different than press releases not being discoverable by web searches, but rather attacks the whole cottage industry of manipulating search engine results through posting of press releases on PR websites. eReleases and its partner PR Newswire, along with the many hundreds of media partner sites that stream their press releases, instituted a policy of "no follow" links more than a year before this announcement.

Web 2.0 involves greater connectivity and user-generated content.

Press releases have been marginalized and maligned as they lost their original intent: to reach the media with a newsworthy idea designed to trigger a journalist to write an article. This unique article, which if posted online, can include a relevant link to your company or website. This creates the natural, organic types of links that cannot be bought but are earned through well-written, strategic, and newsworthy press releases.

An Introduction to SEO and Web 2.0

Web 2.0 is a concept that was introduced in 2004. Since then, it has been discussed, debated, denounced, and revived. It has been talked about as if it could be a revolution in how the Internet works and batted around as an extraordinarily popular buzzword. One reason behind its tumultuous history is that it has a definition that is both unclear and constantly changing. For our purposes, we will discuss Web 2.0 from the perspective that it is the term used to describe the tools and utilization of Internet-based programs that lead to greater connectivity and user-generated content.

The Internet is largely a passive experience. You go to a website, look at the content it provides, then move on to the next website. You might be able to leave a review for a product on some websites, but largely, the website and the user operate independently from one another. Web 2.0 describes the tools and practices that move the Internet away from that model. Now there are many sites, tools, and programs that allow typical users to generate the content that people consume. (Remember that content is king and that the goal of every press release is to become publicly available content.) With these tools, users don't create all of the content, but they can create a great amount of it, and they also have a greater say in what content is consumed by other users.

In effect, Web 2.0 allows for a great democratization of user-controlled and user-generated content; it puts users in control of information. For an example, think of the online encyclopedia Wikipedia, which is written and edited entirely by users.

Search Engine Optimization (SEO) is not intrinsically a part of Web 2.0, but it is a process that can utilize Web 2.0 to great advantage and lead to a greater online presence and potential returns. When done properly, SEO can put the right contact in front of the right eyes at the right time. This is a key concept, and to discuss it further, let's take a step back and examine some basics.

Search Engines

Search engines are the Internet's information gateway. When you know you need to find specific information but don't know exactly where to find it, you search for it with a search engine. After you enter a word or phrase into the search field, a search engine will display the results, which are pages of links that are relevant to the word or phrase you specified.

For a simple video overview of search engines and how they work, watch this short video entitled "Web Search Strategies in Plain English" by Common Craft: http://tinyurl.com/CCSearch.

On a search results page, the three most important factors are location, location, and location.

Web results are listed in an order that is called a "ranking." Ideally, the first website listed in a search result would be the most relevant to the terms of your search. Even though these results aren't numbered, they are still listed in order of importance, and that importance is based on a number of factors. Few people know all of those factors, but a number of them are known, and using them to your advantage is what SEO is all about. Make no mistake, the position of a website when searching for a phrase is no accident.

Think of a search results page as real estate: The three most important factors are location, location, and location. There are typically only ten results per page for any search — ten out of hundreds of thousands. Most people never click past the first page. Many go only as far as the first link on the page. With that said, if you have a company that sells Super Widgets, and you sell your widgets through your website, how important do you think it would be for you to make sure that your website is the first one to appear when anyone in the world does a search for Super Widgets? If the first thought that came to mind after reading that question was anything other than "extremely important" it is time to re-evaluate your business acumen.

SEO

As mentioned, Search Engine Optimization is the process of optimizing content, like a website, so that it is treated favorably by search engines. SEO is the key to making sure that your information shows up at the top of the search results page. SEO is not an exact science. There are many strategies to take into consideration when optimizing a website for favorable ranking; some are easy enough for almost anyone, while others require the expertise of a specialist. But there is still plenty that can be done on a novice or intermediate level that will help tremendously, and that is what we are going to cover.

An SEO press release must appeal to both users and search engine robots.

Writing SEO Press Releases

When writing an SEO press release, it's important to note that the old rules still matter. Even if you are bypassing journalists to appeal directly to customers online, you aren't advertising or marketing. Press releases, in any form, are still public relations. So take the already understood guidelines for proper press release writing and use them as a baseline for SEO press release writing. Especially in an online environment, you want to present your business professionally and show respect for your intended audience.

To write an effective SEO press release, take your baseline understanding of press release writing and enhance it with SEO-specific necessities. The best first step when starting an SEO press release is realizing that it is more than just a press release — it's a web page. Sure, you can write it on a word processor and it will seem like any old press release, but the intent of an SEO press release is that it will be posted online and will have to compete for traffic and attention like any other post. Accordingly, an SEO press release must appeal to both users and search engine robots.

Writing something in a way that appeals to search engines, as well as using tactics that appeal to them, is the optimization part of SEO. Optimization requires knowing what search engines look for and rank highly in response to a search query. Some of these optimization techniques can be written right into the text of a press release, while others require a more technical approach to the website where an SEO press release appears.

When writing an SEO press release, there are two optimization considerations of particular importance:

- Keyword Optimization
- Originality/Authorship

There are many other matters to consider in the grand SEO scheme, but these two are the most important strategies that almost anyone can implement, and they don't require overly technical explanations.

Keyword Optimization

When people do searches online, they may think that they are searching for "how to write a press release," but what they are really searching for is a string of keywords.

Tailor the press release so it will rank highly when someone searches for its keywords.

Keywords are critical because businesses, blogs, etc. want to be inextricably associated with them. In fact, it's best to think of keywords as another form of branding. If you do a search for "books," for example, the highest ranked sites are Barnes & Noble, Amazon, and other sites that are obviously attached to books. The more keywords that you use, the more specific the results become. If you expanded your book search from "books" to "rare books," then the first results may be AbeBooks, Alibris, and BookFinder, all sites that are more specifically geared to rare books, rather than books in general.

These specific sites rank well in search results because they have been keyword optimized. Keyword optimization consists of identifying those keywords that best correlate to a press release/website and tailoring the press release/website so that it will rank highly when someone searches for those keywords. Alibris doesn't have to try to rank for "books" because the company knows that its customers are looking for rare books rather than for books in general.

There are, however, two problems that every business out there has to struggle with: which keywords to use, and competition for keywords.

Choosing Keywords

When choosing keywords, it's best to start with the obvious: What does your business do? Do you sell algebra study guides for high school students? Great, then you should definitely be considering "algebra study guide" as a set of keywords to focus on, but don't make this decision alone.

There are a lot of keyword tools out there that can help you determine the best keywords to use. Of them, the Google AdWords Keyword Tool (available for free here: https://adwords.google.com/select/KeywordToolExternal) is probably the most widely used. (See also Wordtracker's free keyword tool at http://freekeywords.wordtracker.com.)These keyword tools provides suggestions and metrics on keywords that people are searching for based on a keyword or phrase you entered.

When you enter "algebra study guide" you will notice that there are a lot of people that are searching for that keyword phrase, but there are also a lot of searches for just "algebra guide," as well as guides for specific algebra levels, like "algebra 1 study guide." You will also notice that there are other similar search phrases that people aren't searching for as much. After browsing through the options, you might want to consider the keywords that not only work best for you, but the ones that are still competitive without being overcrowded. After all, the idea isn't just to rank for something; it's to rank for search terms that people are actually using in their searches.

Choose two to three keyword phrases for optimizing your press release.

You don't have to choose a single keyword or keyword phrase to rank for, either. You can attempt to rank for anything that is pertinent to your business because it will help to bring in greater traffic. Ideally, it is best to choose a set of two to three keyword phrases to optimize your press release because anything more might come across as spammy to the search engines. The key is to incorporate these phrases in the body of your press release while maintaining the balance of appearing natural. Don't forget that there are other people trying to rank for the same keywords, creating a competitive environment for the most influential keywords.

Don't pursue keywords based solely on search volume. It's quality over quantity — with a dash of grounded expectations. While the keyword "study guide(s)" is searched for an average of 2.5 million times a month, it is useless to optimize for this keyword as you are unlikely to break the top 10 results in any search engine based solely on a press release. You stand a much better chance with a three-word or four-word phrase like "algebra study guide" and "college algebra study guide." If you bid on keywords through PPC, like Google Adwords, review the keywords that convert for you. In addition, review your keyword results in the search engines. If you rank on the second or third page of results for a keyword, it shows you have a stronger likelihood of bumping that result than starting from scratch.

Keyword Competition

Everyone wants his or her business to be successful. Even if it's not possible, an entrepreneur wants to be "the source" for whatever it is he or she sells. The reality for small- and medium-sized companies, however, is that there is always someone bigger. Now, there's nothing wrong with that, but it is something that you have to take into consideration when dealing with keywords.

For SEO, consider three-word and four-word keyword phrases.

Let's say that you sell computers. Trying to rank for the keyword "computers" is fine, but there are a lot of other companies out there that will rank higher than you no matter what (e.g., Dell, Apple, Toshiba, etc.). So while it's ambitious to try and rank for "computers," your results will likely be insignificant. The other sites bring much more to the table in terms of inbound links and credibility, making it hard to compete head-to-head on a one-word keyword.

One of the reasons why researching keywords is so important, beyond telling you what people are actually searching for, is that it gives you suggestions for keywords and keyword phrases that are still competitive but not impossible to reach. One standard suggestion is to look at and consider three-word and four-word keyword phrases. They are usually specific and easy to rank for — and they are closer to the way people actually search. So consider being more descriptive with your keywords. Instead of relying on "computers," think about "cheap notebook computers" or "discount desktop computers." Keyword tools will suggest numerous three-word keyword phrases based on the keywords that you search for. If you have a keyword phrase already in mind, make sure to research it with a keyword tool before optimizing for it.

The more words in a phrase that you are optimizing for, especially after three, the more likely it is that you'll rank for it, but the less likely that someone will actually search for it. This means it's probably very easy to rank for a keyword phrase like "South Carolina die cast car model outlet retailer," but the likelihood of someone searching for that phrase is minimal. It would be more difficult to rank for "die cast car models," but that's something that people would likely search for.

Optimization

Now that you've taken the time to find out what keywords work best for optimizing your SEO press release, how, exactly, do you use those keywords in a way that gets results? The answer to that is glaringly obvious: Use the keywords! A lot.

Keep in mind that search engines like Google are just computers running algorithms. They aren't unintelligent, by any stretch of the imagination, but they aren't human, either. If you search for a particular set of keywords, a search engine is going to look at all of the places where those keywords show up online. Now, there are literally hundreds of factors that go into why something is ranked like it is in a search result. But having a specific set of keywords appear frequently is a strong start.

So when writing your SEO press release, or just optimizing your website, if you are trying to optimize for a particular keyword or keyword phrase, include it as many times as you can naturally fit it in. Natural word flow is for human readers, but keyword repetition is for the search engines. A properly optimized press release probably mentions an optimized keyword between four and a dozen times in a way that seems relatively natural to readers. To reap the maximum benefit of keyword optimization in a press release, make sure that the keyword appears in the headline and has at least one instance of anchor text (defined and discussed later) in the body.

Robots don't understand context.

When speaking to someone one on one, we have a tendency to use shortcuts with our language; otherwise, our discourse with friends and peers would be cumbersome and annoying. So it's quite expected that in most contexts, conversations are objectively vague while being completely understandable to humans. This cannot be the case for something that is being written for SEO. Robots don't understand context or slight variances in words that humans would understand. If you are trying to rank for "desktop computer," you have to use that phrase as much as possible and resist the urge to use "desktop PCs," "desktop machine," or "full-sized computer." Of course, do this in a way that still seems natural to readers. Just keep in mind that to search engines, "desktop computer" and "desktop PC" are two entirely different things.

See this example of a keyword-optimized paragraph that frequently uses the keywords "discount," "desktop," "laptop," and "computer." It uses keywords in a way that is beneficial to both readers and search engines.

Discount Computers is your best source for high-quality discount desktop and laptop computers and computer supplies. When you use Discount Computers, you can be assured you are getting a sturdy, well-built discount desktop or laptop computer that will last for years. Our extensive assortment of desktop computers, laptop computers and computer supplies makes shopping for your next discount desktop or laptop computer a simple and pleasant experience.

Unfortunately, this can be abused very easily, and because of that, search engines crack down on sites with excessive use of keywords, a practice known as "keyword stuffing." Typically, those who keyword-stuff know they are doing it and do it maliciously. It takes the form of huge blocks of text that are full of randomly repeated keywords that are typically hidden from users, but not search engines.

So when writing keyword-rich content, don't worry about being mistaken for a keyword-stuffer as long as you are writing responsibly. Or, as Google puts it in its guidelines, "focus on creating useful, information-rich content that uses keywords appropriately and in context."

Technical Details

There are also some extremely technical considerations for using keywords in an SEO press release. Of the hundreds of variables that Google uses to determine a website's importance and rank, there are some that Google considers to be more valuable than others, and those require specific know-how.

Search engines like plain text.

To start off easily, search engines like plain text. There is a lot of content on the Internet that is prettier and more visually appealing for humans, like using images or video for content, but search engines have trouble viewing those. To most search engines, an image or video just looks like an address for a file (http://www.website.com/media/file.jpg). So while your users might think it's really cool to have a video overview of your business that they can watch, search engines can't access any of that content, so any clout that the content within the media could have in helping a website rank goes completely out the window.·

A good example of this is using pictures as links to other pages on a website. Say, for instance, you have a website selling many different brands of fountain pens (Waterman, Parker, Monteverde, etc.), each brand getting its own internal webpage on your website. As a retailer, you would like to rank not only for "fountain pens" but for the individual brand names as well. But instead of listing the different brands in text on the main page, you decide to use clickable images of the pens as a link to that brand's internal page on your site. This may help customers who know by sight the kind of pen that they like, but even if the brand name is written on the linking picture, your website won't receive much ranking benefits from the keywords on the pictures, even if you use ALT and TITLE attributes. So if it's important in any way, make sure to have it written out in plain text so that search engines can read it.

Another technical consideration is that search engines typically place more value on website elements that are designed to signify importance.

There are a number of elements that every website has or can use to signify that certain items are more important that others. To optimize these elements, you have to know what they are and how to use them effectively.

Title Tag

At the very top of every web browser there is an area where a website's title tag is displayed, and it usually says the name of the website. Google and other search engines consider this area extremely valuable. So when working on a webpage, it's equally important that the webpage's title tag effectively uses the keywords that the webpage hopes to rank for.

Every page on your website, including your press releases, should have an appropriate title tag that accurately describes the information that can be found on that page. These accurate descriptions need to contain the keywords you are attempting to optimize for each respective page. Also, while using a website's name in the title tag is always a good idea, for anything beyond the main page, the unique title of a page should precede the website's name. For instance, the following would be the html coding of a properly ordered title tag for a page on a particular variety of teas at the website TeaFanatic.com:

```
<title>Roasted Asian Teas — TeaFanatic.com</title>
```

Meta Tags

Meta tags are not typically seen by users, as they are coded into each page's head tag. Search engines, however, can see them easily and sometimes use what is written in them when displaying results.

The two main meta tags that a site should use are the "keywords" and "description" tags, which are where you write out each page's individual keywords and descriptions, respectively. Not only is this a good way to position a few more instances of your most important keywords, some search engines might use your description meta tag and actually display it in search results to assist users. While Google definitely uses the description tag, there is debate in the SEO community whether the keywords tags are used at all by the search engine company. Here is how the meta tags for the page we've already considered would look in the html coding for that page:

```
<head>
<title>Roasted Asian Teas — TeaFanatic.com</title>
```

<meta name="description" content="A listing of some of the most delicious and aromatic roasted teas from Asia. Roasted teas are an Asian speciality, but most Westerners aren't familiar with their unique flavors. TeaFanatic.com gets you pointed in the right direction.">

<meta name="keywords" content="roasted asian tea, roasted tea, asian tea, tea, tea for sale, tea list">

</head>

Anchor Text

Anchor text is text that is clickable because it has a link embedded in it. You probably see it on almost every website that you visit (usually as "click here"), but it is especially prominent on news websites and information hubs such as Wikipedia. There, in almost every entry, if there is a reference to something else that has a Wikipedia entry, it is linked with anchor text so that you can click on it and go straight to that article.

Anchor text is still text, so it is easily readable, but it is also especially important text because it is linking to another web page. What it tells a search engine is, "Hey, we are talking about XYZ here, but if you really want to know about XYZ, then you have to go to this other website …." In press releases, you can use anchor text to link to specific pages on your website, or to other press releases. Doing this should help to build your ranking for the keywords that are used as anchor text.

Anchor text points a search engine in the right direction.

To a search engine, anchor text is like a road sign pointing the engine in the right direction. The more signs there are, the more confident the search engine will be in taking that direction.

Like everything in SEO, this can be easily overused. As with the caution against keyword-stuffing, some people use excessive anchor text in an attempt to find favor with search engines. This is frowned on and could lead to a negative impact in search rankings. But also like the keyword-stuffing caution, using anchor text responsibly in a way that is intended to benefit your users is perfectly acceptable.

In terms of ranking, having other sites link to yours is a better way to achieve ranking, but it doesn't hurt to link internally as well, which means from one page within your site to another page within your site. And like everything keyword-related, be specific with the text that you turn into a link. Using "click here" or "this article" as anchor text is just wasting a perfectly good opportunity to add some weight to a keyword phrase.

Heading Tags

A word that is written within a heading tag is more significant (in the eyes of a search engine) than the same word written outside of one.

Heading tags are little bits of code that are used to denote titles, headings, and so forth. They usually increase the text size of whatever is written within them and make the text bold. Just as you would write the title of an article in bigger font to set it apart from the rest of the text and gain readers' attention, heading tags are a pre-coded way to format text to set it apart and indicate its importance. Search engines, when determining page rank, will assign more importance to words written in heading tags. There are six levels of heading tags, from header one (h1) to six (h6), with header one being the most important.

In SEO press releases, the headline is usually written within h1 tags and a subhead is written within h2. The same can be done with most website pages. Here is how a heading and subhead would appear in html coding.

```
<h1>TeaFanatic.com Announces New Selection of Premium Roasted Asian Teas</h1>
```

```
<h2>Roasted Asian teas are the pinnacle of gourmet teas, offering rich, smokey flavors and new experiences for tea lovers.</h2>
```

Originality and Authority

Originality and authority are both vital elements of page ranking, and even though they are two different attributes, they often walk hand in hand.

Originality

Originality is a plain and simple element: Is the content you have written original or has it been duplicated from something else? Duplicate content occurs when multiple webpages, either on your website or on other websites, have content that is largely the same. It doesn't mean that the content is identical, but it is so similar that there is little reason to differentiate between the pages. Duplicate content can be a serious issue online because it can be used counter-productively to try to force page rank. More often than not, though, businesses just don't realize that they are using content that is duplicated. This leads to search results that that aren't preferable. Google lists a few examples of content that are often unwittingly duplicated too frequently:

- Discussion forums that can generate both regular and

stripped-down pages targeted at mobile devices

- Store items shown or linked via multiple distinct URLs
- Printer-only versions of web pages

Duplication can be an issue because Google values (and ranks) original pages significantly better than duplicate ones. If there is a set of of websites that contain the same content, Google will do what it can to determine which one came first, thereby establishing it as the author and originator of that content, and then Google will assign that website a higher rank.

In cases where you have too much duplicate content within your website, Google's robot might be forced to make a decision on which of the multiple pages to show, and it may not show the page that you want displayed in search results. That's because Google wants to be able to give users relevant content when they search for something; Google will choose one of the many duplicate pages and display only the one it thinks works best.

The major concern this introduces to website owners is that it takes the control of what content users see out of the hands of the website owners and puts it in the hands of the search engine robots. However, this concern can be eclipsed by the fact that if there is too much duplicate content out there, it "confuses" the search engine robots and causes a website's ranking to plummet. So the ultimate repercussion of having too much duplicate content is that your page won't rank in any competitive way and the page that ultimately will be displayed may not be the page with the information that the user is looking for.

To avoid duplicate content, write original material in a unique way.

The best way to avoid duplicate content is to write original material in a unique way. Some companies have a standard template for their press releases and will simply alter the important information so they can save time and not start every press release from scratch. While that's never really a recommended practice, it is a tremendous mistake for SEO press releases. A good rule of thumb for writing an SEO press release is that the only thing that should be shared between press releases is the company boilerplate. Everything else should be written from scratch.

A major factor affecting duplicate content that is out of your hands is other websites that duplicate content entirely. This can be a problem. Some websites, like news aggregators, may duplicate a press release in an attempt to share the information, but some malicious websites duplicate information to bolster their own authority and attract substantial user click-through, which generates advertising income. Usually, if a site duplicates something entirely, the duplicated webpage will show up later in the search results than an original would because the original has the benefit of originality. Nonetheless, if the site duplicating the content has a huge amount of authority, it could trump the original in a search result.

This can be devastating for some websites because it can translate to a real loss in advertising income, but it is not as worrisome with press releases. If an SEO press release is widely duplicated to the point where the original ranks lower than the duplicates, it just means that the press release is still ranking highly and has content and links that point to and benefit your website, so there is no measurable loss. In fact, inbound links are the most likely outcome of an SEO press release, and if your press release is published in only one place, the links can stay tremendously focused, which adds a great deal of authority to the press release's webpage and to the website as a whole.

For a more thorough, and more technical, explanation of duplicate content and how to alleviate its penalties, read Google's short help guide at: http://tinyurl.com/DuplicateContent.

Authority

There is a fundamental difference between traditional press release distribution and SEO distribution. With traditional distribution you are trying to disseminate your press release to as many potentially interested people as possible. With SEO distribution, you put your press release in one place online and have it optimized so that the people who would be interested in its information can find it easily with a search engine and come to it. The main reason for keeping a release in one online location is the originality and authority issue. Now that you know how originality words, let's look at authority and how it relates to originality.

When we are looking for information of any kind, we are always looking for it to come from some authority. The importance we place on the information determines how authoritative we prefer the source to be. For most situations in life, it is easy to determine the level of authority someone or something has, whether by a degree, resume, tenure, notoriety, etc. But this pedigree process doesn't translate easily to the Internet. So how is authority determined in a place where the rules are entirely different?

We mentioned previously that search engines are basically robots. More precisely, they are a set of algorithms that look at a huge array of variables to determine the importance of a website. This importance is known as the website's authority, and most of the variables that are measured are industry secrets. However, the biggest known factor for determining a site's authority is how many inbound links the site has.

Inbound links are hyperlinks from a person or website that link to your website. The idea is that if a website has good content that people find relevant, people will talk about it, and other, well-respected websites will link to it. The more inbound links that a website has from recognized and quality websites, the more authority it has.

The rules for inbound links have grown over time.

For a while, the rule for inbound links could be easily summed up as "one link, one vote." So for every inbound link you had, the more authoritative your site would be. But this was very easily abused, so the rules for inbound links have grown over time. Among the numerous tweaks, link popularity is a key factor in inbound linking. With link popularity in play, not all links are equal and the authority determined by inbound links becomes a derivation of the quality and quantity of the inbound links and the sites from which they originate. So now, not only does the number of links come into play, but the authority of the site that is providing the link counts as well. So an inbound link from a well-established website would carry much more authoritative value than an inbound link from a small blog without much influence.

One of the ways many sites would build up inbound links was by having people post on message boards and leave comments on blogs and other social media websites. This easily and quickly turned to spam, but it is usually not an issue anymore. Today, most areas where users can leave comments are coded with a "nofollow" attribute, which alerts some search engines not to take hyperlinks from such comment areas into account in page ranking.

Posting comments on blogs and social media websites is still a good idea, though, as long as the comments are not spam. In the next section we will thoroughly go over the different social media outlets and discuss how they can be indispensable for your business, but because of the "nofollow" attribute, there is no free lunch for comments and inbound links. Even though placing a link to your website in the comments area or message board of another website won't allow you to leech off the authority of that website anymore, your website can still experience a measurable benefit from those comments and links. If you write thoughtfully and responsibly while commenting on another website, then the benefit that your website will experience will be through people who are impressed with the quality of your feedback and who will visit your site on their own accord.

Distributing SEO Press Releases with Social Media

Social media includes blogging, Twitter, Facebook, MySpace, LinkedIn, Digg, Flikr, and many other interactive sites. It is a Web 2.0 mainstay, and it serves as a primary way for a business to distribute information (including SEO press releases) on the Internet. Social media, in itself, does not have an immediate effect on page rank, but it does have an impact on the visibility of information. One of the unique attributes of social media is that the amount of visibility that a piece of information experiences is entirely dependent on the person distributing the information and how much other users like that information.

The basic idea behind social media is that it focuses on people and explores different ways to put people in touch with each other. It gives users outlets that allow them to share information in ways that haven't existed before. People, not companies or organizations, are the ones in control of content and they can tailor it to meet their specific needs. This doesn't mean that users can fully change the news or make things up, but they can choose the news that they think is important and shine a spotlight on it, no matter how obscure. With tools like RSS feeds, which bring the latest updates you've selected right to your desktop, and social bookmarks, which indicate what other people have found interesting, you can look at only the kind of news that you are interested in without having to search through all the traditional media outlets.

For a simple video overview of social media and how it works, watch this short video entitled "Social Media in Plain English" by Common Craft: http://tinyurl.com/CCSocial.

Social media also encourages people to form and join interest-based communities where they can easily branch out and find new sources of information about which they hadn't previously known. These communities are exceptionally powerful and influential because they are communities of real people and enthusiasts who operate on a very interactive, person-to-person level, which builds up a communal trust. So when a respected member of a community shares some information of interest, other members of the community are more likely to look at or consume the presented information because of that pre-existing trust.

The goal of any effective online PR campaign concerned with distributing SEO press releases should therefore be to become an active, trusted member in the communities where your information matters or is of interest. To do that, you should share your information along with any other information that is relevant or of interest to your participating community. Showing that you are a real person with real interests outside of the interests of your company is the only way to build trust in an online community, and it is the only way to distribute your information effectively.

Keep in mind that there are more than a handful of social media websites on the Internet, and some may have multiple appropriate communities for your business. When looking at all of the options that are available for social media sites, and the amount of effort that has to be invested to become a truly accepted member of the community, it can seem like a daunting task — but your reward is a highly focused audience. It is a basic business principle that you should appeal to the core of your audience since you know it is already interested in what you are selling. The same is true for the communities that are built into social media. Many of these social media sites have highly specialized and niche communities that you can join. For many businesses, this means that they won't have to build an audience entirely from scratch. These communities are highly focused, pre-built audiences that businesses can tap into as long as they can become trusted members of the community.

Become an active, trusted member in the communities where your information is of interest.

As time goes on, social media will only play a bigger and bigger role in business, so savvy entrepreneurs would do well to start participating as soon as they can. There are a lot of advantages to using social media tools, including increased website traffic, making new business acquaintances, and introductions to potential customers. It all starts with the one factor that active participation in social media can guarantee: visibility.

SEO press releases, just like all PR efforts, require building visibility within a community, and that requires a significant amount of time and commitment. With traditional press releases, a steady flow of press releases and a consistent PR campaign is required to build recognition among journalists and interested parties, and the same thing is true of social media communities. You can't be a stranger putting out a press release and hope to have social media communities immediately lavish attention on you and spread your information. You have to spend time with these people and become their friends; only when you are a recognizable presence in a community will your information be treated as something more than corporate advertising only worthy of being ignored. You can't reap the benefits without putting in the work, but if you do invest the time and energy, there can be some very tangible results.

The following is a discussion of the most common business outlets for social media. There are a number of them, and they all play a slightly different role in an overall social media presence. While blogs and Facebook are probably the most actively used, each of these social media sites comes with its own value — and again, with social media, the more you put into your chosen outlets, the more you are likely to get from them. In these next sections we will explain what these social media sites are, how they work, and then touch on the kind of role they can play in the distribution of SEO press releases. After covering the individual websites, we will discuss how to use them in an overall social media campaign, and how SEO press releases fit into the bigger public relations picture.

Blogs

Did you ever have a journal as a kid — one where you wrote down your thoughts on the day or just ranted about the things that were going on in your life that you felt you couldn't tell anyone else? That's kind of like what a blog is, or at least that's how blogs started — only your "journal" is online, and everyone can see it. My blog on PR marketing, which attracts more than 10,000 first time visitors a month, can be found at: http://www.ereleases.com/prfuel.

Blogs started out as personal online journals, but the medium quickly morphed into something more substantial and respected. They still have that journal format; however, instead of entries, you make posts, and instead of writing down personal secrets, you write out news, information, articles or opinions that you want people to read. While there are still people who have blogs that act like a journal, today they are used by just as many businesses as a way to discuss their industry. They are also considered to be a good source for alternative news and analysis. No matter how they are used, one of the main benefits of a blog is that it is an easy way to create your own content.

For most businesses, there are two very good uses for blogs. First, a business can use a blog to discuss industry-related things. The most successful business blogs take a look at the business' audience and determine the various interests that the typical audience member has. They then post information and write entries that may include information about their business, but mostly they focus on stories that the audience will like.

Blogs started out as personal online journals.

For instance, say you have a company that sells exotic fruit. Your company's blog should certainly contain information about new products and sales — in other words, any business information that would be beneficial to your customers — but you can't write about yourself all the time. For your blog to be more appealing, you should write about your customers' other areas of interest, such as cooking, recipes, travel tips, or anything else that someone who likes exotic fruit would deem valuable enough to search for that information online. Even if it is a business blog, staying away from a single focus is the best way to interest customers and keep them coming back. Since the blog normally isn't the main purpose of a business website, blogs on business websites are known as "value-added content."

The second good use for a blog is that blogging software offers a great platform for publishing search engine friendly content, like SEO press releases. Now, it should be said that if you have a regular blog like the one described above, you shouldn't use that same blog to publish press releases. Though they both use blogging software, the two fulfill very separate purposes and should not be intertwined.

If a business does not have an area already set up for press releases in a newsroom on its website, using a blog to post press releases is not a bad idea. Blogs are very search engine-friendly by default, and most blogging platforms, like WordPress, offer downloadable extensions that can enhance the way things are posted so that they are more SEO-compliant as well. Also, blogs are easily indexed and searchable, making it simple to find and reference previous press releases.

If you operate a blog, you usually have two communities that you should be concerned with: the community of people surrounding your specific blog, and the larger community of multiple blogs known as the blogosphere. It's essential that you participate in any community that might arise from your own business' blog, but it is also highly recommended that you participate in the blogosphere at large as well. This means posting and participating on other blogs that you like, whether they are related to your industry or not.

Blogging software offers a great platform for publishing search engine friendly content.

Any blog can sprout a community because all blogs allow people to read posts and comment on the post. This area is known by many names. Though it is often just called the comments area, it is sometimes called a "TalkBack." The more people that comment on a post, the less like a series of comments a TalkBack becomes, and more like an ongoing conversation. And with the right amount of information bringing in the right number of comments starting the right number of conversations, a community of regulars may form soon enough.

A good way to drive people to your business' blog is to participate in other blogs frequently and become a member of the blogging community. If you participate frequently and have good things to say, then other commenters may naturally follow a link back to your blog (which you should provide when signing up to participate in a TalkBack). If these other commenters like what you have to say on your blog, then they might become regulars, or they might link to your blog on their own. Either way, the more you participate in other blogs, the more possibilities you create for others to find their way back to your blog.

Another way to drive people to your blog is to take contrarian views on a particular subject or industry practice. When everyone within your industry says something that is recognized as standard industry practice, more people will take notice of the person who asserts that this is the wrong thing to be doing. For example, a blog post with the subject "Why Going Green May Destroy Your Business … and Hurt the Environment" may attract a lot of attention as "Going Green" seems to be a subject that is hot and widely supported. A contrarian blogger could pick apart the downfalls of being on the cutting edge of technology within an industry, stating that the high costs of implementation at this stage could lead to severe losses for a company. By extension, these losses could result in layoffs and an underutilization of the equipment, thereby resulting in inefficiencies and a waste of resources this equipment was meant to combat.

Become a member of the blogging community.

Your blog should eventually be the cornerstone of your business' online presence and SEO distribution strategy. Blogging is the best place to do things on your own terms, and blog posts have the added benefit of being content that you can later share through social media communities. Everything that you do online — every account that you have on every social media site — should have a link that points back to your blog. It couldn't hurt to have links from social media site to social media site, but having everything link back to your blog is essential. Social media is all about spreading the word, and it is crucial that even if you aren't blatantly sharing information about your business, you are spreading access to your blog and your business.

For a simple video overview of blogs and how they work, watch this short video entitled "Blogs in Plain English" by Common Craft: http://tinyurl.com/CCBlogging.

And for further reading on how blogs can play a part in a greater PR strategy, check out these PR Fuel articles:

http://tinyurl.com/PRFuel-PRTools

http://tinyurl.com/PRFuel-ValueAddedContent

http://tinyurl.com/PRFuel-OnlinePresence

http://tinyurl.com/PRFuel-BlogTraffic

http://tinyurl.com/PRFuel-SuccessfulBlog

http://tinyurl.com/PRFuel-BuzzBlog

RSS

RSS stands for "Really Simple Syndication" and, as the name states, it is a simple electronic syndication application. Electronic syndication may sound complicated, but it really isn't, and that's important to know because it serves as a backbone to a significant amount of social media. So let's take a step back and explain exactly what RSS does.

Syndication means the distribution of content through multiple channels. Much of the media that we experience every day is syndicated: Comics and articles in newspapers, TV sitcoms, and popular radio shows are frequently syndicated. Even though he writes for *The Miami Herald*, for years you could read Dave Barry's column in hundreds of newspapers because it was syndicated. Charles Schulz didn't work for any particular newspaper or company, but his comic strip, *Peanuts*, ran in almost every newspaper in the country through syndication. So you see, syndication is a way to enjoy content via numerous outlets. RSS performs the same function specifically for web content.

Here is an example that helps illuminate this concept: There is an industry blog out there that you really like to read, but it isn't updated consistently. You want to know when it is updated because you like commenting on its articles and posts. So to stay up-to-date with this blog, you would have to check it periodically to see if there is any new content. Since the updates are intermittent, sometimes you forget to check, and you come to a conversation late in the game. Or you keep checking and get frustrated because there aren't any new updates when you wish there were. But, if this site had an RSS feed, your problem would be solved.

With RSS, you can subscribe to any blog or website that has a feed and have new content delivered to you, rather than you having to seek it out. But first you have to have an RSS reader. An RSS reader is a program that collects the RSS feeds that you subscribe to and presents those feeds to you in one place. There are dozens of different kinds of RSS readers out there. Some are programs that you download to your computer, others already exist in web-based services like Google, and many other e-mail programs like Apple Mail and Microsoft Outlook provide RSS readers.

Once you have a reader, all you have to do is go to your favorite websites and subscribe to their RSS feeds. Then, instead of going out to all of those websites to see if they have updated, all you have to do is go to your RSS reader and any new content will be there for you to read, all in one place. Now isn't that convenient?

Of course, this isn't just convenient for you; it can be convenient for all of your customers as well. Every special feature of your website, especially your blog and your SEO press release center or newsroom, should include the option for users to subscribe to RSS updates. With RSS, subscribers are aware of any new content that you post and any new SEO press releases that you publish. This can build a more active flow of information between you and your customers.

And finally, as mentioned earlier, RSS is the backbone of a lot of social media programs. While it doesn't work exactly the same (it's not a notification in a reader), the RSS structure is what most social media programs, like the ones about to be discussed, use to notify large groups of people and turn them into communities. The RSS technology is what gets the word out from one person to another, and through countless personal networks.

For a simple video overview of RSS, including a re-cap of how it works and some details on how to set up a RSS reader, watch this short video entitled "RSS in Plain English" by Common Craft: http://tinyurl.com/CC-Syndication.

Facebook and Social Networking

Facebook is a social networking website. There are many other social networking sites out there (most notably Twitter and LinkedIn), but Facebook is proving itself to be the most prominent and the most rewarding for both people and businesses.

Social networking sites basically serve as a way to keep in touch with people and talk about the things you find interesting, including with people you may not have met in real life. Even if you haven't thought about it, everyone has a social network. You are connected to the members of your family and your friends and acquaintances, and they are connected to their family, friends, and acquaintances as well. Right under our noses we have a huge network of people that we scarcely think about, but we should because these networks are powerful.

RSS is the backbone of a lot of social media programs.

What social networking sites do is help us explore existing person-to-person networks and start new ones, though it isn't as systematic as that makes it sound. Basically, you start a profile explaining who you are — a little background information, where you work, what your favorite books and movies are, etc. Don't worry, though: no one sees your details unless you let them — once you've mastered Facebook's ever-changing privacy settings.

After you have a profile, you locate the profiles of your friends, colleagues and family members. This way you are actually setting up a virtual model of your social, familial, and business networks. Once you are friends with someone, you will receive updates on what he or she is doing. You can see new pictures that have been uploaded, notes that have been newly entered, and activity status updates so you can know what he or she is doing at the moment. And of course, your friends can all see the same information coming from you.

Another feature is the ability to join "groups." These groups are networks that users create about a specific topic. There are literally thousands of topic-based groups , ranging from fan groups for a band to places for serious discussion on certain political issues. The members of these groups are sometimes friends offline, but they are often collections of people from all around the world who have never met in person but are now bound by their interest in a topic and their membership in a Facebook group. In these groups you can meet new people and form friendships with people you know share an interest with you because they took the time to join a particular group and participate in its discussion.

Social networking sites help us explore existing person-to-person networks and start new ones.

At this point, you may be wondering how this applies to your business and PR in general. The answer to that is simple: create a fan page for your business. Fan pages differ from groups in that these are publicly viewable, allowing unregistered users and search engines to view the content. Instead of making a personal profile, make a business one with a personal touch. After all, people don't really want to interact with something inanimate or conceptual — they want the personal touch and to feel like they are making a connection. So combine your business and your personality and make yourself known.

Invite business acquaintances and other members of your industry to become fans of your page. Join groups and become fans of pages that are relevant to your business or initiate one if there isn't one already. Participate in discussions and make new friends from groups and pages. Even if you don't establish a formal friendship with someone, frequent participation will raise your profile, and if other members like what they read, they will probably look at your profile, group, or page, which can all direct visitors to your business' website.

When you post a new SEO press release, you can announce it to your broad network of friends. You can talk about it in your groups if it is something that is pertinent to the conversation. If the site where you publish your SEO press releases has an RSS feed (and it should), then you can set it so that the feed of any new press release will be turned into a note on your profile, allowing anyone who can see your profile to read your press releases as they are published.

Of course, with these activities, as with pretty much everything in public relations, there are no guarantees. But good PR helps create possibilities, and the more you participate in social networking, the more possibilities you are creating for potential business contacts and customers. And since services like Facebook have over 150 million active users, a number that is continually growing, there are certainly ample opportunities accessible to you.

For a simple video overview of social networking and how it works, watch this short video entitled "Social Networking in Plain English" by Common Craft: http://tinyurl.com/CC-SocialNet.

Twitter

Twitter is a unique entity. It's somewhat like blogging and somewhat like Facebook, but certainly not a clone of either. To define it more accurately you could say that it's an "express" version of social networking centered around a micro-blog.

Just like other social networking sites, you create an account and connect with friends, colleagues, and relatives. But you don't have to stop there. There are a lot of interesting people that you can follow and keep up-to-date with on Twitter. Unlike other social networking sites, you don't have to submit a friend request that your friend has to approve. Though the setting can be changed on that, generally anyone can follow the updates of anyone.

Announce a new SEO press release to your broad network of friends.

Unlike regular blogs where you can write whole articles in a post, Twitter limits your posts to a mere 140 characters. What's the point of that, you say? Well, the basic idea behind Twitter is that it is a way to keep people up-to-date on the little things. All Twitter entries (called "tweets") are supposed to be an answer to the question that is listed at the top of each Twitter account: "What are you doing?" Of course Twitter can be, and is, used in more ways than that, but keeping people up-to-date in 140 character intervals is its primary function.

One of the biggest advantages that Twitter offers beyond its original intent is that based on its format, it can be more like a conversation than other social media. Tweets are short and there are often lots of them, so there is a natural back-and-forth that happens on Twitter. Of all the opportunities that this provides, customer feedback and Q&A are some of the best.

There are many major companies out there using Twitter as a corporate communications tool these days, and out of all of them, the grocery store chain Whole Foods is considered to be a shining example of a business using Twitter the right way. The Whole Foods company "Tweeter" answers questions that other Twitter users ask, as well as tweeting links to posts on the company's blog, links to articles, and plenty of other bits of information that aren't necessarily related to Whole Foods but would be of interest to Whole Foods' costumers — such as tips on green living and unique recipes. All of this comes together as a massive and direct communications effort between the store and its customers.

Many businesses just look at Twitter as a way to tweet the headline of their latest SEO press release, but that approach can inadvertently prevent people from following your business. While you certainly can tweet about your latest press release, don't do it incessantly or in a way that will disrupt the conversational flow of tweets. The majority of your tweets should not be self-serving links to your own site but rather be links or snippets of information of interest to your core group of followers. Once you've established a reputation as a provider of useful information, you can leverage that connection by incorporating links to your own press releases, blog posts, etc.

Twitter can be more like a conversation than other social media.

Another benefit is that you don't have to follow people or have them follow you to know if they are talking about something that you would like to discuss. You can subscribe to RSS feeds of particular Twitter searches so that any time someone tweets something that you are interested in following, you will know about it. Then you can use that as an opportunity to answer a question, introduce yourself, or just help out in whatever way you can.

It's all part of the open communication and community ideas that thrive in today's online culture. And that's why Twitter is such a rising star in the social media community. In other social media sites like Facebook, you have to be someone's friend, be in a group, or monitor a fan page, to follow the topic threads of your preference. For Twitter, the focus is on the conversation, and almost anyone can drop in and join that conversation.

For a simple overview of Twitter and how it works, watch this short video entitled "Twitter in Plain English" by Common Craft: http://tinyurl.com/CC-Tweet.

Pinterest

There's no denying the meteoric rise of Pinterest. The little social media site that could went from humble beginnings in early 2010 to the third biggest social network on the Internet earlier this year. Considering the hundreds of various social media sites out there, it's a pretty big deal! Users treat their profiles like giant tack boards and attach stuff they love to let others know what they like. Then, like-minded people connect through shared interest. How easy is that?

Ever since Pinterest launched (and certainly since it started to blow up), companies worldwide have been trying to grab any customers they can from the site. However, it's not like Facebook where you can directly market and talk to people – Pinterest is all pictures all the time, and they're not fond of obvious business pandering.

One of the main questions to consider when going after an audience is whether or not they'll even care about your company at all. Big brands like Lowe's have tried to go after the Pinterest market with mixed results – the real numbers have yet to be seen. But as the Pinterest user base tends to skew towards artsy and DIY focused people, some companies will have more trouble than others.

The other aspect to consider is the "visual" nature of Pinterest. Since it's all pictures, you have to rely on photos to drive people to your real website and storefront. If your business doesn't have any sort of photo presence (i.e. products, physical accomplishments, etc.) it's just not going to work. If you're an accountant, posting pics of paperwork and money clips probably won't get the job done.

Some companies (usually smaller ones) have reported that they've seen a jump in traffic since they started work on their presence on Pinterest. However, there's one notable issue: so far, it seems to be just traffic and not sales! The bounce rate for Pinterest links has skewed higher than other links of the same nature thus far, indicating nobody is staying around to buy anything.

Of course there's no real reason to not at least try and bring in some new blood with a Pinterest campaign – if you have the time that is. If you have a brilliant strategy to rope users in to your accountant business using pictures, go for it. You never know, it could work.

But I do suggest just trying out a sampling first. Putting in too much effort could not only drain your energy but time you could have spent elsewhere. And again not every company out there is good for Pinterest, just like not every business works on Twitter or LinkedIn.

Just because something is a hot new trend doesn't mean you have to jump on it. If you can make it work, go for it, but until real data comes in from the few forerunners it's tough to see where the real money is.

Digg

In today's information-based society, there is so much information being generated and news occurring every day that it can almost feel like a full-time job just to keep up with the latest issues and stories. Digg provides a unique way to stay current with the news that most people feel is worth your time. Digg is a news aggregator social networking site that is very different from the ones that we have already discussed. It's different because it isn't so much concerned with people getting in touch with people as it is people getting in touch with news.

Digg is a news aggregator social networking site.

The way it works is simple. At this point almost every news story, article, blog post, picture, and video on the Internet has a Digg button next to it. If a person with a Digg account sees something that he or she likes and wants to share, all he or she has to do is click the Digg button and vote for it (otherwise known as "dig" it, get it?). The more Diggs something accumulates, the more visible it becomes, leading to more people viewing it and possibly more Diggs. The main Digg website lists news stories, blog posts, and any other kinds of Digg-able media that are just starting to get attention as well as those dug items that are most popular or just hitting "critical mass." Like most news sites, there is a main page that lists recently popular Diggs as well as topic pages for subjects such as technology, politics, and so on. This way you can look exclusively at the kind of news that interests you.

But don't forget that Digg is also a social networking site. As a member, you can comment on the items that are being dug and make friends with other Digg users. Just like all other social network sites, Digg has a community, and since it has targeted topic areas, there are a lot of people that specialize in certain subjects. The communities are an ideal way to build relationships and network. After a while you will probably know enough people that they will Digg your content and you can Digg theirs. That way you can help each other build visibility.

Delicious and StumbleUpon

If you have a computer and have ever used the Internet, it is all but a certainty that you know what a bookmark is. For a web browser, a bookmark acts the same way as a real bookmark, in that you can mark a page for quick and easy future access. Like Digg, Delicious and

StumbleUpon are focused around people finding interesting websites and voting on them in a way that shares them, but unlike Digg, these social bookmarking sites allow you to categorize and customize the sharing of sites by including sorting tools like tags. Delicious and StumbleUpon are the most popular and widely used social bookmarking sites.

Every social bookmarking site collects your bookmarks on a personalized page, but with Delicious and StumbleUpon, when you add that bookmark to your page, you can personalize the bookmarked page's description and attributes. You can tag the page with keywords so that you know exactly what the site covers and so you can easily find it later. As soon as you start tagging your bookmarks, you have an easy way to reference them for the specific information that you need.

You can tag a page with keywords.

Let's say, after a while, you have collected a significant number of bookmarks of a wide variety, and you want to look at the bookmarked websites focusing on a certain topic, say web development. All you have to do is click on the "web development" tag that you have placed on the appropriate sites while you were saving them. The website will then bring up only those bookmarks that are tagged as having something to do with web development. Not only does this make accessing information easier for you, but anything that you tag as "web development" will be added in with all the other pages that other users have tagged as "web development." This is one of the ways that these services are social.

Every bookmark that you create is collected on a single webpage for you, but all of your bookmarks are also all viewable by the public. Every time you bookmark something and tag it, it adds to the greater community of bookmarks. If you bookmark something that other people have bookmarked, it gets a quantity of votes, just like on Digg, increasing the visibility of that particular bookmark.

Like all of the other social media sites, communities are key for social bookmarking. It is easy to see who is bookmarking what and to see if they have the same interests as you. The more you participate and share, the more visibility you are giving yourself with both individuals and a community.

For a simple overview of social bookmarking and how it works, watch this short video entitled "Social Bookmarking in Plain English" by Common Craft: http://tinyurl.com/CC-SocBookmarking.

Whenever you distribute a press release, you have the opportunity to "share" it on any of a dozen or more social bookmarking sites or social media networks. Do take advantage of that option if you can, especially for sites and services especially frequented by you and your target market.

SEO & Social Media Play Guide

As previously mentioned, self-distribution through the use of social media websites is the best way to drum up attention for your press release and establish the kind of presence and authority for your SEO press release that will make it visible for future users.

Now that the individual social media websites have been discussed, let's look at how they should be used for establishing a sustained online presence, of which the distribution of an SEO press releases is but a part. Even if your interest in online media is purely for SEO press release distribution, it would be a shame to squander the various benefits of a robust online presence by approaching that presence with a narrow purpose.

At this point, you should know that presence and visibility are a necessity for SEO press release distribution, but the more the Internet becomes ingrained in our society and in the ways we live and work, the more presence and visibility become necessary for business as a whole. So when we go over this section on how to use social media as a proper means for the distribution of information, don't just think of it in the limited terms of SEO press releases; think of how it can be used as a way to expand your business and meet the new expectations of content consumption.

Establish and cultivate your online presence in a very personal way.

To utilize SEO press releases and social media to their greatest capacity, you have to establish and cultivate your online presence. You do this by becoming involved in the various communities that blogging and social networking provide. But unlike what most businesses might expect, you have to get involved in a very personal way. After all, it is called "social media" for a reason.

The tendency that most business have when deciding to use social media outlets as business outlets is to treat them all as sales opportunities. They never "turn off" and are always trying to work some angle. When it comes to social media, this approach is antiquated; simply put, it will not work. It may seem like a paradox, but when using technology that is encouraging people to keep in touch in a virtual medium, personality is treated as currency. In other words, the sterile facade that most businesses construct as their professional image is completely worthless when you are entering an arena where people want to get to know other people. The more personality that is exuded in social media, the more that personality can connect with and relate to the larger network of personalities.

When getting involved with social media, you are attempting to become a member of a community that is already established; in essence, you are a guest. If you think of it like that, it's easy to see how jumping in, trying to sell something to people you don't even know, and generally acting like you own the place are actions that only the most boorish of guests would take. If you are a guest in a community, you have to act like a guest and ingratiate yourself with the community until you are accepted as a member.

Becoming a member of a community takes time, just like any PR campaign, and any SEO distribution strategy involving social media should be thought about in the long term. When entering the blogosphere and any (or all) of the various social media communities, it is well worth your time to sit back and learn the ropes through observation for a little while. Online communities have cultures just like real-life ones do, so it couldn't hurt to get a feel for each place and the people in it to see if that place is the right fit for you. Sometimes, finding the right place with the right people can be just as important as finding the right keywords for your website.

How Social Media Communities Work

It's hard to say exactly where to start when establishing an online presence via social media communities. There is no road map to becoming a social media expert, so you should really start where you feel most comfortable. Maybe that's Facebook, maybe it's Twitter, or maybe just start finding other blogs that are similar to yours and start commenting there.

With social media, you build rapport by sharing content.

Think of all the social media communities that you belong to as one large party. You don't go to a party and start talking business to everyone. Instead, you mingle, have a good time, and talk business every once in a while when it comes up. If you go to a party and you want to have a good time, the key is to participate, to talk to people, to engage them on a human level. Even if you barely know these people, you are building bonds, establishing networks and a vital level of trust and acceptance. You do the same thing when you are interacting with people in social media communities.

You can't actually speak with these people in the communities, so how are you supposed to "mingle" as outlined above? With social media, you build rapport by sharing content and discussing it in TalkBacks. If you see an article that you really like, why not Digg it? Then go and comment on it in Digg. Maybe something happened in your industry that is huge, and a lot of people are trying to understand it. Write an article on your blog explaining it. There's a chance a lot of other people are writing similar articles, so go find other blogs that are doing the same and comment on them. Maybe you agree or disagree; either way, talk to the other commenters and share your point of view. Along the way, why not link to your article as well?

After you have started following some major players in your field on Twitter, read what they are talking about and write to them every once in a while. Maybe you can build a relationship. If you see someone asking something that you can answer, feel free to do so or point that person in the direction of the right information. If it happens to be something that you have written about, feel free to use that, but it's OK to point in someone else's direction. Encourage customers, or anyone, to ask you questions on Twitter, where you can get back to them quickly.

The more you get involved with the communities, the more you will understand how information flows. If you find a website that is a good resource, then bookmark it on a social bookmarking site. Use the social media icons that you can find next to almost any content on the Internet and share that content in a manner that you see fit.

To go back to the party analogy, you may not be talking to someone at the party who needs your services at the moment, but that person might need you down the line. Or maybe this person knows someone who will need your services later. If you are doing what you can to make an impression, people will remember you when the time is right. Maybe someone saw one of your bookmarks on StumbleUpon and liked a lot of the sites and stories that you linked to. Then this someone found out that you have a business selling a specific product, The person has no need for your product, but he or she likes your blog and reads it periodically. Months later, this person may have a friend who tweets something like, "Anyone know a good place to get X?" Then this person, who found out about you because of the sites that you bookmark on StumbleUpon, is in the position to act as an advocate for your business. And all the while you may never have met or heard of this potential advocate.

But it doesn't stop there. What if the person who was looking for your product tries it? Sure, you got a sale, but what happens if your customer likes your blog, too — and even follows you on Twitter or mentions your business on Facebook?

Certainly there are a lot of variables in these scenarios, but that is how human networks operate. They aren't always exact, but the more connections you have, the more possibilities there are out there, and that is the basis for public relations. And the more social media sites you belong to, communities you join, content you create, and comments you make all lead to a greater increase in possibilities.

How Social Media Communities Work for You

What we have discussed so far in the social media section of this book is basically an online utilization of public relations. It is a way to show how creating possibilities may not guarantee instant success but can lead to results over time. Now let's talk specifically about how social media can be used in concert with SEO press release distribution.

To put it plainly, you can post your SEO press release on every social media site that has been discussed, though you probably shouldn't put every press release on every site. That would work against the social nuances that we have been touting. But we have mentioned that using social media to talk about your services is fine in moderation, and Tweeting, Digging and StumblingUpon your SEO press release is something that you should do as long as it's not all that you do.

Facebook will alert every one of your friends or fans to a new press release.

We have emphasized joining communities and raising your visibility. These actions are good PR moves. They increase your online presence and connect you to other people. And while this is great for PR, another advantage is that when you eventually Digg an SEO press release, or StumbleUpon it, or make a Facebook note out of it, not only will a lot of people see it but they will be people who are part of your main target audience.

If you have it set up so that any SEO press release that you publish on your website gets placed on your Facebook profile or page through RSS, then Facebook will alert every one of your friends or fans. When you post it on Digg, the people you know on Digg might Digg your release if you have a history of Digging something of theirs. You can even mention it on your blog and tweet about it on Twitter so that all of the people who follow you on those sites will know about it. This expanded network of people is a very powerful tool, and it is one that you can use only if you connect with people on a personal level and don't compromise their confidence in you by trying to sell them your products or services all the time.

Having your SEO press releases distributed through social media also brings the benefit of visibility. It goes without saying that social media tools allow an SEO press release to be visible to a large group of people.

In addition, there is search engine visibility.

It has been mentioned in previous sections that the trade-off in using SEO press releases over traditional ones is that you forego distribution of your press release to journalists in an attempt to appeal directly to consumers. In order to do that, you put your SEO press release online, do what you can to make it visible to search engines and rank highly. You then hope that when someone is searching for the kind of information that is present in your press release, he or she will see your press release and use your product or service because of it.

We have encouraged you to build and maintain an online presence and to use social media because it will draw people to your business and provide you with an avenue for distributing your SEO press releases. The more people you know and the more communities you are involved in means the more potential eyes that can be looking at your press release. But keep in mind that there is a benefit to search engine visibility with social media as well.

When you propagate information using social media, it is just like creating an inbound link for that site. And as you recall, inbound links are one of the most important factors that search engines use to establish a website's authority and give it rank. So every time someone Diggs or bookmarks your press release, that acts like another inbound link pointing to your press release. And of course, the more of those you have, the better ranked your press release should be.

Keep in mind that if you want a lot of people to spread your press releases via social media, the two best things that help are good content and having a strong presence in a community (or communities) interested in the kind of content that you provide. So write well and be social.

PR, SEO, Web 2.0, and the Bigger Picture

People still value the legitimacy and weight of the media.

Based on all of the information that has been covered in this chapter so far, there is no doubt that this new avenue of public relations has many facets and can impose a steep learning curve. Using the Internet and all it has to offer for a completely new public relations strategy is, without a doubt, a new frontier. But while the trend is toward modernizing, changing, and embracing the digital, the old is not falling into obscurity. Traditional press releases are modernizing and keeping up, remaining just as important for the business-press-public relationship now as ever.

There may be a time when the relationship among businesses, consumers, and the media becomes so drastically different that press releases become obsolete, but that day is not imminent. A likelier scenario is already occurring where press releases are reaching bloggers as legitimate members of the media. Now and for the foreseeable future, people still trust the media. People still value the legitimacy and weight they bring to a subject, even if consumers now obtain their news from an online version of a newspaper — or even a blog —instead of the real thing. And until that changes, press releases will always serve as a needed liaison between a business and the media in the hopes of spreading the word.

SEO press releases are not usurping the mantle of traditional press releases — they are existing alongside them. This means that you have a choice to make in your public relations strategy. With any choice like this, there is always a trade-off. (While you can do both, newswire distribution means lots of duplicate content spread across dozens of websites, which could easily complicate carefully prepared SEO plans.)

Now a press release is only a search away from your target audience.

Public relations is all about creating possibilities. There are never guarantees, but there is the knowledge that without those possibilities, there is little to no hope for opening up opportunity. When deciding between SEO and traditional press releases, the question you have to ask yourself is, "Which will create the most possibilities for my business?"

With traditional press releases, you are writing for journalists about something that will appeal to your audience. You work for and hope to score good coverage, and from that coverage you hope for better sales. However, when you send out a traditional press release, there is no guarantee that journalists will use it, or, if they do, they may use it in ways that you didn't expect or want.

SEO press releases more or less eliminate the middleman, putting a press release only a search away from your target audience. You write a press release and put it online. The more it is optimized, the more paths you clear between the users and the release. But just as with traditional press releases, there is no guarantee that your release will rank well. You can do what you can, but sometimes there are just too many big players in the field. Or, if you have done everything you can (i.e., used good keywords that are competitive and gained exposure through social media sites), your press release will likely still be only one bit of information that the user will consider.

One of the strengths and weaknesses of putting so much power in the hands of users is that they are doing more decision-making than ever. Where there used to be a vetting process by the media, now your information is out there in the raw and it will be subject to greater scrutiny. There is little to separate your information from the countless other bits of information out there. You can do what you can to stand out, and there is a lot to do, but in the end, you may still be just a drop in an ever-expanding ocean.

The good news, which may sounds contradictory to what you just read, is that press releases work no matter how you use them. For some goals the traditional route may work best, for others, the SEO route. What matters most in your public relations strategy will always be the quality of your content and the amount of time and dedication you are willing to put into your PR efforts. Note that a single press release is never a public relations campaign. You must dedicate a series of press releases over a period of time to carefully evaluate what works and to tweak your messages. At a bare minimum, a company should issue at least four press releases a year. So as long as you have something that is really worthy of the public's attention, and you are willing to do everything it takes to be competitive in the PR market, then you are bound to gain something in return.

What kinds of topics are newsworthy?

1. New product or service

2. New website or significant upgrade to existing website

3. Involvement with charity work

4. Making a charitable contribution

5. Free shipping offer or change to shipping rates

6. Releasing findings of new study or research

7. Helpful tips related to your business

8. News of the weird (e.g. Coffee shop offers excusive $200 gourmet drink)

9. Commentary on or tie-ins to current events

10. Interesting trends

11. Starting a new sister company

12. Receiving an award

13. Being singled out for an accomplishment

14. Offering free information: ebook, newsletter or white paper

15. Celebrating an important company anniversary (e.g. 50 years in

business)

16. Opening a new office or relocating your office

17. Changing the company name

18. Changing a product name

19. Signing a large, well-recognized client (make sure you have their permission to publish this)

20. Announcing a media appearance

21. Inspirational stories of overcoming major challenges

22. Hosting a seminar or teleseminar

23. Sponsoring an event or team

24. Partnering with another business or organization

25. Hiring a new executive or changing ownership of the company

26. Announcing personnel change: retirement, resignation or death

27. Changing the way your products are made

28. Changing the prices of your products or services (particularly if you're reducing prices)

29. Developing a new technology or unique procedure for your industry

30. Rebranding your business

31. Reorganizing your company

32. Hosting a major contest, sweepstakes or promotion

33. Making an outrageous claim (be careful not too sound to gimmicky or salesy)

34. Revealing industry scams

35. Announcing holiday-related sales and events

36. Making predictions for your industry

37. Provide expert opinion on important subject within your industry (think sound bites when creating quotes in your announcement)

38. Publishing findings of a recent report, survey or poll

39. Filing of a lawsuit

40. Responding to being name in a lawsuit

41. New uses for your products

42. Receiving endorsements from a major celebrity or public figure (make sure you have their permission to publish this)

43. Offering internship program with local schools

44. Establishing a scholarship

45. Hosting a tour of your facilities

46. New certifications and credentials achieved by your staff

47. Providing pro bono work

48. Responding to accusations against your company or industry

49. Setting a major goal

50. Launching a referral rewards / affiliate program

51. Speaking at a conference or event

52. Providing free consultations or a free sample

53. Taking major steps to go "green"

54. Debunking common myths

55. Taking your company public

56. Discontinuing a product or service

57. Filing or Being Awarded a Patent

58. Merger or acquisition

59. Celebrating an important milestone (e.g. one millionth customer)

60. Exhibiting at a trade show

61. Stock offering

62. Financial or earnings update

63. Securing business funding or credit (e.g. VC or angel investment)

64. Tips sheet or feature story (e.g. Top 10 Valentine Gifts, Effective Tips to Land a Job in 30 Days, Turn That Brown Lawn into a Suburban Oasis)

Section 4:
Expectations, Reality, and the Aftermath

Chapter 11

What Happens After You Distribute a Press Release

What Comes Next?

Once a press release has been distributed, the issuer has no real control over what happens to the information. This is part of the risk and beauty of press releases.

We have already mentioned how there is a trade-off in public relations. In advertising, you can say almost anything you want, any way you want, and you can aim directly at potential consumers. That just isn't the case for press releases. You have to aim for journalists, tailor information to their needs, and say what they want the way they want it. It's not easy, but there are benefits to using PR over advertising because of its greater legitimacy.

News has three times more credibility and six times more readership than paid advertising.

According to Starch Research, news has three times more credibility and six times more readership than paid advertising of equivalent size. No one trusts advertisements to be truthful or have consumer's best interests in mind. On the other hand, press coverage acts as a filter of credibility for consumers. If something ends up in print, on TV or the radio, that means a professional somewhere thought that particular information was important enough to be worth people's valuable time. That's the power of content.

Still, once a press release is distributed, what happens to that information is up to journalists and other press release recipients. Even though the business that distributed the press release cannot control the release once it is in the hands of others, there is still work to do, and it helps to know what to expect.

Setting Realistic Expectations

There is an expectation that a release will do all the work, garner lots of attention, and easily achieve the desired outcome. But no matter how well-written a press release is, sometimes it will bring little to no coverage. The only way to counteract that is to treat the press release as an introductory step in an ongoing PR campaign. Only through ongoing press releases will you build the exposure and establish relationships with the media that allow for eventual media pick-up.

There are a few bits of reality to keep in mind when issuing a press release:

1. Members of the media receive dozens, sometimes hundreds, of releases each day. That means competition for a press release even to be read is fierce, which is why we emphasize such a concise focus on the impact of information throughout this book.

2. Information may not always be used in its entirety. The media may use the information in a press release at its discretion, omitting points that the sender of a press release hoped would be highlighted, not including information from studies, or leaving out other details.

3. Articles derived from or including information from a press release may not always be flattering or reflect the image a press release intended to convey. A press release offers information at the risk it will be subject to both praise and criticism.

4. Sometimes press releases may simply not be used. This is often not a reflection on a public relations practitioner. The truth is that sometimes, even if an announcement seems really important, the media may disagree. Or even more likely, there is just too much else going on and the information either wasn't noticed or had to get passed up in favor of bigger stories.

These are just some of many reasons why press releases should be part of an ongoing PR campaign. It's almost a certainty that one press release won't do the job. And even if it gets attention, there's no guarantee that it will be the kind of attention that is desired. Of course, it is the purpose of this e-book to provide all the tools necessary for your press release to have the best shot possible.

Monitoring How a Press Release Is Used

When good coverage comes about it can be a huge benefit for a company. Many businesses like to collect clippings and links to their media mentions. Good coverage can be used to generate more good press. If anything, keeping up with good press allows you to know that people out there enjoy what you do. The biggest problem with that, though, is knowing who, if anyone, has written or said anything about you.

A clipping service is the primary resource businesses use when they want to keep up with media coverage. Clipping services monitor all or a portion of print, broadcast and online media and can provide clippings, links, files, and other documentation that allow for permanent archives of media stories.

While using a clipping service may be a great way to know what people are saying about your company, these services can come at a tremendous cost. The costs for the three main types of clipping services (print, broadcast, and online) can vary, but each could easily be an economic burden for businesses with smaller PR budgets. Broadcast and print, in particular, can run well in excess of $2,000 a month since these clips still have to be compiled in large part by hand.

Online clipping services are a little cheaper since they are compiling links and largely using preexisting search networks. Basic services can start at around $300 a month, but for more tailored reports, like links to blogs that discuss your press release or company, prices can reach up to $1,000 a month. eReleases offers its customers access to its MediaClipping™service (http://www.ereleases.com/mediaclipping/) for a modest monthly fee.

Online clipping compile links largely using preexisting search networks.

The bottom line is that clipping services are a valuable commodity, but for most small and medium-sized businesses, they can be a heavy drain on a budget. Thankfully, there are ways to obtain limited information similar to that provided by a clipping service, but for free.

Google Alerts is a good program that acts similarly to an online clipping service, though it's not quite as accurate. It is a free service and allows users to set up e-mail or RSS alerts for search terms in different categories. For example, if you have set up an alert for the name of your new product, Google then notifies you with the relevant link each time that name shows up in the news coverage it follows. Because of duplicate content issues Google Alerts picks up less 10 percent of most press release postings. To track limited use of press release information, set up a Google Alert for a few key terms from your press release, like company and brand names.

Another option is even more simple: Ask customers where they heard about you. If you do business online, add a field to your online contact form where customers can explain how they heard about your product or service. The same holds true for orders taken over the phone — just have the operator ask the customer where he or she heard about the company while on the line.

Out of Your Hands

We mentioned earlier how the information in a press release can sometimes be used in ways that are unexpected or unfavorable. While this does happen, it should not deter you from distributing press releases. Dealing with media coverage that is good, bad, or just way off the mark is all part of a healthy relationship with the media. In fact, many small businesses have seen an uptick in business after being plucked from obscurity through unfavorable media coverage. There are two things always to keep in mind when dealing with the media after distributing a press release:

1. Always be prepared.

2. Keep your cool.

You may not glean answers from everyone who does business through you, but many businesses have found that if you simply ask your customers, they will tell you where they heard of you. From those responses you can fairly accurately account for the media coverage you are receiving and track down sources from there.

A technical possibility for online businesses is to monitor web stats and server logs to determine the sites from which your visitors originated. Often you can then determine whether those sites used your press release and/or wrote about you.

First, though, let's take a look at an example of how information from a press release can be used in a manner different from its intentions.

Press Release: The newly redesigned Lithium-ion battery can hold a charge for up to 10 hours with regular use and can be fully recharged in 45 minutes.

News Article: The claim is that the new battery will last 10 hours on a single charge, but these lengths are seldom true as advertised. "Regular use" varies from customer to customer and according to a footnote on the company's website, "regular use" means 50% brightness, web browsing, and no use of energy intensive programs or activities like watching DVDs, editing pictures, or playing games.

Since the system hasn't been released yet it's uncertain whether or not the battery can live up to this claim, but it's doubtful since few ever do. When the system is released and tested, it's likely that it will still have admirable battery life, but when put to the test of actual "regular use," it will fall short of its claim.

This is a mild, but realistic example. Journalists are more interested in analysis and giving consumers what they need to know than rubber stamping what a business wants them to report. But there are times when coverage isn't just an analysis of the information provided. Sometimes coverage can be excessively negative, misleading, or just plain wrong.

When this happens, that's when you have to spring into action.

Always Be Prepared

Before you do anything else, take a cue from the Boys Scouts and be prepared. Depending on the kind of information, there could have been a number of things that led to an article being written the way it was. Regardless of the reason, though, make sure that you have the proof to counteract whatever negative claims were made. That way you can insist on a retraction or a corrected article, or you can put out a press release correcting the inaccurate information.

Keep Your Cool

Obviously, negative coverage is never welcome, when the intention of a press release is to promote its subject in a favorable light. When that happens, an immediate response is crucial. However, it's paramount that you keep your cool, no matter how bad (or good) the situation is. Reporters are often met with screaming and yelling from PR people who are upset at the way their information was portrayed in an article; all that does is hurt professional relationships. Instead, think of bad PR as an opportunity to create good PR.

If there is a bad article out there, get in touch with the journalist, talk it over with him or her and express your views and concerns in a professional way. If the situation is bad enough that it needs rectifying, then take care of that in a similarly professional way. Afterwards, offer the journalist an open invitation to get in touch with you in the future with any thoughts or concerns he or she may have.

For further reading on these issues, see these articles:

http://tinyurl.com/PRFuel-KeepingCool

http://tinyurl.com/PRFuel-FreakOuts

http://tinyurl.com/PRFuel-FailedRelease

On Achieving Maximum Effectiveness

No matter how it is distributed, the success of a press release begins with how well it is written. Although the media can take a release and do with it what they will, there are still a few things that public relations practitioners can do in assuring their releases achieve maximum effectiveness.

Always make sure that the press release leads backs to you. This involves the inclusion of relevant information about when an event will be held, where a product can be purchased, why people should respond to the information, etc. It would be a serious flaw for any press release not to list a website.

- Know the importance of having a presence. While it's important to avoid becoming the "pesky public relations person," public relations practitioners have to make sure that the media and general public know that their organizations exist. Remember that a series of strategically targeted press releases is important to any public relations campaign. Wire services transmit nationally, but make sure to build up local relationships as well.

- Respond to events by issuing press releases that include relevant information about what is happening in the world. However, be careful not to comment about every issue or news item. If a major event can be turned into a good angle for your business, feel free to piggyback on it and enjoy the extra attention that it may bring you.

- Be diligent about the timing of press releases. It makes little sense to issue a press release discussing legislation that was passed two weeks earlier. In doing so, an organization might be targeting the right audience but one that has already lost interest in an issue discussed in the press release.

Chapter 12

What's Next?:

Further Public Relations Possibilities

You've Only Just Begun

Press releases are an opening act: one component of a comprehensive public relations effort. There's still much to be done, even after a press release has been issued, and this chapter looks at where to go from there.

What follows is an examination of how an organization can have a comprehensive public relations campaign. In each instance, the work always goes back to a press release being issued to accomplish these goals.

Having a Presence in the Community

Develop a positive image in the community.

An organization's name may be familiar to the community, but that does little good if it's used only when that organization is promoting only its own interests. An organization can further its public relations efforts by knowing how to publicize itself in a way that wins favor with the community. Developing a positive image involves positioning an organization's name in front of people. Accomplishing the goal of getting an organization's name before the public can involve anything from participating in disaster relief efforts or sponsoring free community events, to partnering with other organizations to support projects that improve life for area residents.

Major corporations often sponsor stages at music festivals across the country. The result is that the mention of their name reminds people of the good times they had at such events.

Each spring, Schaeffer Eye Care Center in Birmingham, Alabama, sponsors a crawfish boil. The event runs two days and features bands playing in the street, food vendors, artists, and other attractions. As a result, people probably think of seafood, live music, and fun with friends every time that they hear the name Schaeffer Eye Care Center. Subsequently, Schaeffer is likely the first place that many people think about when they have a need for eye care.

And how do organizations publicize their efforts in helping with disaster or sponsoring community events? The process begins with issuing a press release about the initiatives.

In 2003, Hurricane Isabel hit an area of the Mid-Atlantic that is not accustomed to experiencing the full force of a hurricane. Of the many areas that were damaged, historic downtown Annapolis, MD was one that experienced unprecedented flooding. After the storm, when hundreds of people returned to their businesses and homes to assess and repair the extensive damage, they were met by employees of Outback Steakhouse, in uniform and driving the corporate Hummer, who were handing out free steak lunches and bottles of water.

Major events don't happen every day, and in the case of disasters, you don't want them to happen at all. But there are countless little things that a business can do to have a presence in the community: sponsor a local play or event, set up a scholarship, have employees volunteer at libraries, food banks, etc. If you want to make the biggest impact, find out what the community thinks is the most important or most needed and go from there. Often, these area of needs can be discovered by talking with your employees who live in the community.

Helping the Media Localize Events

The media are always looking for stories. Sometimes the opportunity to promote an organization may come as a result of events outside the community. Achieve success in this area by keeping up with events and recognizing how they can be utilized in promoting an organization.

The process begins with keeping current on what is happening in the news. Knowing what is going on in local and national politics, government decisions, financial issues, and other news is important. But that alone is not enough. Public relations professionals should also keep up with what is happening in entertainment, fashion, fads, and other current events that may tie into the work they do.

The ways that public relations professionals can help the media localize news are numerous:

1. Research groups can sponsor forums related to issues being covered in the news such as military spending, the environment, etc. By sponsoring these events, organizations not only expand visability of the issues, the accompanying coverage puts their name in front of the public.

2. Are studies being released that address news events? What efforts are being made to promote current events by experts within an

organization?

3. What political and social issues in the news can a policy group or religious organization use to its advantage with commentary, studies, or data examining the issue, etc.?

4. What products does a company sell that could be useful for special occasions, such as high school proms, graduations, or summer vacations? Are efforts being made to let the public know about them by creating ad campaigns, promotional tie-ins or other efforts?

Going Beyond the Media

There are other sources besides the media that an organization can use in getting its message out to the community. From advertisements to community events or promotional items, the options are endless. Working beyond the media also involves remembering the importance of targeting an organization's messages.

If you rely only on the media to spread a message, you risk missing a large percentage of a community. That realization would have held true 10 years ago, and it is especially true today, as fewer individuals are watching television news and the readership for newspapers continues to decline nationwide.

Consider these examples of the right and wrong audiences for a message:

- An area that is largely populated by senior citizens is ideal for promoting services for older residents such as discount prescription plans or retirement communities. But it would be wasteful to spend money advertising those same products in an area that is home to a large segment of college students or young families. The same holds true for direct mail marketing. Are brochures on programs for retirees going to those who are eager to receive them, or to families more interested in the latest clothing for toddlers? And are coupons and advertising subsequently being mailed to those younger customers?

- An advertisement promoting the hottest new clothing or must-have electronics would be perfect in a magazine for young people who normally have disposable incomes because they have not started families yet. But placing an advertisement for children's toys in a publication read mainly by people in their late teens would likely be a waste of advertising money and could even be seen as inappropriate given the issue of teen pregnancy. Most consumers in that age range are not parents yet and are more interested in products for themselves.

Determining the age-specific group for some products is simple, as illustrated by the two examples above. But there are other areas that have to be considered, such as income levels, community trends, racial makeup, etc. All of this information is available from different sources. It's the responsibility of public relations practitioners to obtain such data and utilize it as part of their public relations plans.

Once a decision has been made about a target audience, the next step is to decide what methods would work best in reaching that audience. There are numerous options available, including billboards, radio or television commercials, direct mail, email marketing, magazine advertisements, and promotional items.

Decide which methods would work best in reaching each audience.

The decision on what works best for an organization is something that can only be determined on a case-by-case basis. Success comes with being bold and creative, and not being afraid to fail. Just because something didn't work for one company doesn't mean it won't work for another. In addition to what has already been covered, there are several traditional methods of sharing information that should not be neglected:

- Newsletters, updates, advertisements, or other means of communication that are mailed to supporters, customers, etc.

- Websites with information that is current, relevant, and easy to locate. Telling someone that information is available on an organization's website and then making it difficult to find defeats the purpose.

- Name recognition throughout the community. Judging student competitions, volunteering in community efforts, and partnering in civic programs all help to put an organization's name before the public.

Managing Crisis

Sooner or later, every public relations practitioner will have to deal with a scenario that he or she wishes would just go away. But navigating the waters of a potentially disastrous situation requires more than wishful thinking. Responding to bad news effectively can also mean the difference between success and failure. The biggest criticism of Tiger Woods during his recent marital scandal has been his silence. Silence lets the media craft its message with no input or spin by the accused. It also frustrates and angers the media, further alienating a body that has served as such a valuable ally in the past.

It is bound to happen eventually. One day everything will be going great and, without warning, something will happen that redefines the term "crisis management." While it is often said that any publicity is good publicity, anyone who has ever had to endure a potentially damaging situation would take a broader view. Bad publicity can raise a company's profile and lead to necessary change, but it can also hurt staff, consume resources, and erode years of good work.

- In most organizations, it is usually understood that the public relations person is the contact for media inquiries. This must be emphasized in order to assure accurate information is provided and, more important, that information is not distributed that is not intended for release to the public.

- Being forthcoming with the media is an absolute imperative. But there may be details that need to be withheld regardless, as in situations where proprietary business practices are in question or where deals, like a merger or an acquisition, have yet to finalized.

- Making sure representatives know what is happening keeps them from saying the two words that the media detest the most: "No comment." If an organization can't provide information, explain why (which is different from saying "no comment"). If the media ask for information previously provided, remind them of that in a firm but polite manner. Stonewalling the media can lead to even bigger headaches. And lying is even worse.

- In situations where dealing with a crisis spans an extended period, daily meetings between the public relations staff and executives of the company are also important. Setting a specific time each day to discuss the situation is a must, and it may be beneficial to meet more than once each day.

- As with most situations, whether professional or personal, the reality is often not as bad as the fear. Dealing with a bad situation is not a pleasant experience, but being prepared and honest can help an organization successfully manage the problem.

Snatching Victory From the Jaws of Defeat

Getting the media coverage or community response an organization is hoping for isn't always easy. But less than successful results don't always have to keep an organization from achieving its goals.

It happens to both well-known and less familiar organizations alike: Interest wanes and there is little to no coverage by the media. In the case of companies marketing products, there may be frustration with the realization that what they are attempting to sell the public on just isn't catching the public's interest.

When public interest either falters or fails to catch on, re-examination of tactics may be in order:

1. Is the organization promoting itself in the most positive manner possible?

2. Is the organization's message being communicated clearly? Is it a message the audience will be receptive to?

3. Is everything being done in regard to contacting and following up with the media? Are all possible efforts being made to reach an audience beyond those who read newspapers or watch television news?

4. Is the right audience being targeted?

5. Is there a need for the information or products that an organization is marketing? If so, is information being released that lets consumers know that? Has it been effectively shared that there have been improvements to the products or services that an organization provides?

Defining an Organization

Promoting interest in an organization starts with knowing how to explain its message. An organization's message may be right on target, but it will fall on deaf ears if the message isn't delivered properly. A public relations professional who cannot communicate a message that is focused and consistent is bound to fail. And the opportunities for failure in public relations are numerous:

- An organization cannot reach people if it is not specifically addressing the needs of the groups it represents.

- A new product will not sell unless consumers know how it will improve their lives or fulfill a need.

Public relations efforts succeed only if they perform one or all of these three tasks:

1. Clearly define what the organization, product, candidate, etc. is all about without resorting to discrediting another company or product.

2. Tell customers or clients specifically why the information being shared is best for them.

3. Share information that is consistent.

In regard to the first consideration, marketing a product that only claims to be better than a competitor's accomplishes nothing. The impact is that consumers are left with claims that an organization has made, but they still haven't been told what makes a product superior.

The second consideration ties in with the first. Consumers and clients need to know about an organization. The organization's name may be out there, but what does it stand for?

A consumer can look at a product all day and still not know its purpose if an organization doesn't explain it properly. Breathe Right helped its audience understand its product by tapping the sports industry. Seeing football players use its nasal strips helped familiarize viewers with how the product worked to maintain a steady flow of oxygen.

There has to be consistency in regard to the principles that an organization represents or the product it produces. For a company, the focus should remain on marketing and promoting what it does best, rather than attempting to please everyone. A customer isn't likely to visit a Chinese restaurant to order a cheeseburger.

Create consistency in regard to the principles that an organization represents.

Conclusion

Throughout this book, great strides have been made to explain press releases as thoroughly as possible — not just in a way that tells you how to write a good headline, but in a way that explains what makes a headline good in the first place. Having a robust understanding of press releases means going beyond knowing that exclamation points don't belong in press releases, or that you should use the inverted triangle when writing; it's about understanding why these guidelines exist. Without understanding why something is the way it is, then it is just a rule, and rules can easily be broken.

Understanding why the guidelines are what they are allows you to write and appeal to your audience of readers in a way that has a better chance of producing results than simply following some rules. In short, the more you know about press releases, the better you will be at writing them, and the more likely you will be to have your information turned into content.

It is our hope that with the knowledge contained in this book, you can go from complete press release novice to a person who can deftly write press releases and build strong relationships with the media. If anything, after finishing the book, you should be at the point where you are willing to start writing your own press releases and focusing on your business' larger public relations strategy.

Please do keep in mind that there is no success without failure. We have emphasized in this book, multiple times, that there are many challenges for businesses just starting their public relations efforts. The first press release, be it traditional or SEO, is always the hardest. Sometimes you can get lucky and it will be a great success, but the likelier scenario is that there will be little interest in your first press release. But no matter the outcome, public relations is all about persistence and creating possibilities.

Many companies don't see notable media attention until their second, third, fourth, or even fifth press release. The problem with most businesses that are just starting with press releases is that they try one, and when it doesn't do anything or does very little, they give up and never give press releases another chance. We hope that we have convinced you that giving up after only a single press release or two is not a PR- or business-savvy action.

Press releases do work, and with this book, we have given you all the

You now have all the tools you need to make the best impression on the media as possible.

tools you need to make the best impression on the media as possible. In public relations, there can be no guarantees, but there are no guarantees in business to begin with. But if you follow this book, internalize its advice, and write according to its guidelines, there is no doubt that you press releases will stand on equal footing with the most well-crafted press releases. And in a field where there are no guarantees, having a well-written press release is starting with your best foot forward.

Finally, even though this book was written for the complete novice, it is perfectly understandable if you have a hard time understanding all of it. The fact of the matter is that the book is long and contains what could easily be an overwhelming amount of information for someone who is starting off with no previous knowledge of press releases.

So, if after thoroughly reading this book, you have come to the conclusion that writing your own press releases is not for you, then eReleases would be happy to write your first press release. At eReleases, we have been writing and distributing press releases for more than a decade. Whether you need a professional to write your press release for you — or you have written your own and are simply looking for a low-cost distribution service that includes newswire distribution, Internet visibility, and media targeting — just visit http://www.ereleases.com and it would be our great pleasure to help your business in its public relations endeavors.

About eReleases

eReleases (http://www.ereleases.com) was founded in 1998 with the idea that press release writing and targeted press release distribution shouldn't be priced out of the reach of small- and medium-sized business owners. The company's website features tips and resources for visitors who want to learn more about press releases, including how to write and distribute their own press release. eReleases also publishes a blog titled PR Fuel (http://www.ereleases.com/prfuel/) that showcases advice and articles on all things PR.

eReleases offers press release writing (http://www.ereleases.com/write.html) and press release distribution (http://www.ereleases.com/submit.html) services. A breakdown of media outlets included in the distribution service can be found here: http://www.ereleases.com/lists/.

Additional features included with each press release submission:

- ·Company eNewsroom™
- ·Newswire distribution through PR Newswire
- ·National distribution to subscribing journalists
- ·Free industry targeting of your press release distribution
- ·SEO enhancements for your press release
- ·Two levels of editorial review
- ·No membership fees, no commitments
- ·WireWatch™ proof of press release distribution

Client results, including links to view each customer's winning press release, can be viewed online: http://www.ereleases.com/testimonials/.

Free 10 Minute Coaching Call

Schedule a free consultation with a Senior Editor.

- Not a thinly disguised sales pitch, but the best intelligence our Senior
  Editor can supply.

- Strictly limited to a 10-minute phone call.

- Use for assistance with press release ideas.

- No commitment & no obligation to purchase anything.

  Sign up: http://www.ereleases.com/freeprconsult.html